P9-APM-695

Connecting Informational Children's Books with Content Area Learning

Related Titles of Interest

Helping Students Learn to Write Poetry:
An Idea Book for Poets of All Ages
Joyce C. Bumgardner
0-205-26169-8

The Right Book, the Right Time: Helping Children Cope
Martha C. Grindler, Beverly D. Stratton, and Michael C. McKenna
0-205-17272-5

Best Books for Beginning Readers
Thomas G. Gunning
0-205-26784-X

Developing Reading and Writing through
Author Awareness: Grades 4–8
Evelyn Krieger
0-205-17355-1

Poetry across the Curriculum:
An Action Guide for Elementary Teachers
Aaren Yeatts Perry
0-205-19807-4

Children's Books in Children's Hands:
An Introduction to Their Literature
Charles Temple, Miriam Martinez, Junko Yokota, and Alice Naylor
0-205-16995-3

For more information or to purchase a book, please call 1-800-278-3525.

Connecting Informational Children's Books with Content Area Learning

Evelyn B. Freeman
The Ohio State University

Diane Goetz Person
Long Island University

Allyn and Bacon
Boston • London • Toronto • Sydney • Tokyo • Singapore

177779

Credits

Series editor: Virginia Lanigan
Series editorial assistant: Kris Lamarre
Marketing manager: Kathy Hunter
Advertising manager: Anne Morrison
Manufacturing buyer: Suzanne Lareau

Copyright © 1998 by Allyn & Bacon
A Viacom Company
Needham Heights, MA 02194

Internet: www.abacon.com
America Online: keyword: College Online

All rights reserved. No part of the material protected by this copyright notice may be reproduced or utilized in any form or by any means, electronic or mechanical, including photocopying, recording, or by any information storage and retrieval system, without written permission from the copyright owner.

Library of Congress Cataloging-in-Publication Data

Freeman, Evelyn B. (Evelyn Blossom)
   Connecting informational children's books with content area learning / Evelyn B. Freeman, Diane Goetz Person.
      p.   cm.
   Includes bibliographical references and index.
   ISBN 0-205-26753-X
   1. Content area reading. 2. Education, Elementary. 3. Children's books. 4. Interdisciplinary approach in education. I. Person, Diane Goetz. II. Title.
LB1050.455.F74   1998
372.41´2—dc21   97-6661
                                                                          CIP

Printed in the United States of America

10 9 8 7 6 5 4 3   01 00 99

For my sustaining connections:
Harvey, Rachel, Naomi. EBF

For the connections in my life:
my grandchildren, Liya and Yonatan,
and my special angel. DGP

Contents

177779

Preface

Welcome to the lively world of informational children's books! Much excitement is happening in children's book publishing today in the informational book area, or nonfiction, as it has traditionally been called. The outstanding quality of these books is acknowledged as more and more informational books win prestigious publishing awards such as the Newbery Medal of Honor book. In 1989 the Orbis Pictus Award was established by the National Council of Teachers of English to honor the most outstanding informational books published each year. These books sing with joy of the stories they tell about lives of ordinary people, of heroes, and of children, too; they tell about great discoveries of our age and small progress painstakingly won an inch at a time.

Today's informational books possess the same lyrical quality and vivid language that young children are accustomed to hearing in their favorite story books. Literary style in both story and informational books is similar, making both genres easily accessible to young readers. The universe is new to every generation of children, and they are eager to explore it and conquer it for their own. With informational children's books they can comfortably read the text and visualize the exciting illustrations; the world is truly at their fingertips, just waiting for them to turn the pages. And we truly enjoy sharing these books with our students and with pre-service and in-service teachers.

The use of children's books in elementary classrooms to teach reading and content area studies across the curriculum is widespread. As professors, the question we are most frequently asked by both pre-service and in-service teachers is not "*should* we use children's trade books" but, rather, "*how* do we use children's books in the classroom?" We have written *Connecting Informational Children's Books with Content Area Learning* in response to that question.

The next most frequently asked question is how to select appropriate trade books that match teaching objectives with children's reading interests and reading levels. Together, we have many years of classroom teaching and public and school library experience. While it is standard practice in literature review journals and other professional publications to assign a suggested or recommended reading level, our combined experience, as well as comments from our students, tells us this is a questionable practice. Most reading levels are based on formulas that count the number of syllables in a random hundred-word text selection. The reader's prior knowledge of the content or interest in the subject matter is not taken into account. The same formula is used to assign a reading level to an excerpt from a fairy tale as to a selection from a science text that may contain vocabulary unfamiliar to most young readers.

We have therefore taken a fresh look at grade level and the assignment of reading levels. While this text is intended for use in the elementary grades (kindergarten through sixth grade), we have kept in mind the unique qualities of every classroom. We know that classes today contain an astonishing mix of children: children who are fluent only in

English; children laboring to attain English literacy regardless of their literacy level in their native language; children who hungrily devour any print media; and children struggling to come to terms with entry-level language skills, for whom books and reading are unfamiliar territory. Assigning reading levels to the books children are asked to read in connection with content area learning is to tell many children they have failed before they start a new area of study; it is labeling them as reading below grade level.

We have tried to select for each of the featured themed content areas titles that represent a variety of reading difficulty, points of view, and aspects of a topic. Some present a brief overview of the content area; others discuss the material in depth. A wise use of trade books is to select a variety of titles so that all children can participate meaningfully in the learning process. It is important that all children find a book to read and participate actively in their own learning while making a significant contribution to the learning cycle.

Reading content area material is different from reading narrative, from reading a story for pleasure, or from reading to learn new comprehension strategies. Children need to be able to concentrate on learning concepts, not just facts in isolation; they should not be interrupted to learn new vocabulary or decode intricate sentences. When you have a variety of trade books available, children can select books they are comfortable reading and can focus their attention on learning new content area material. With several trade books on the new topic, students can read about one aspect of a topic in detail, digest the new material, and then move on to another aspect of the topic. Think of yourself as a reader: When the subject is unfamiliar to you and you have little or no prior knowledge to associate new information with, how do you assimilate the new information? Most of us, adults and children, prefer to select a book that has large, clear type; illustrations that clarify and extend the text; and an uncluttered, inviting appearance. This description fits most children's trade books. Their use allows children to concentrate on absorbing unfamiliar content area material without the necessity of learning new vocabulary or interpreting complex sentence structures. There are many outstanding examples of informational trade books with "picture book" style formats that are popular with all students from beginning readers through middle school and adults as well. Books like these are invaluable for content area learning as well as arousing the interest of curious browsers and reluctant readers. So much of the effective use of trade books depends on how you, the classroom teacher, present these books to your students!

Finally, using informational trade books to teach content area studies allows children to connect with books in new and uniquely meaningful ways. It allows you, the teacher or pre-service student, to think conceptually about how to break down artificial barriers between content studies and "grade-level" reading. With trade books you can concentrate on teaching content area concepts and scaffold children in their search for connections between ideas and information.

In this book's first chapter we explain a rationale for incorporating informational books into content area learning that includes a review of research on children's literature in the classroom, the nature of expository text, the limitation of content area texts, and the use of informational books in an integrated curriculum. Chapter 2 discusses new curriculum trends in math, science, and social studies as well as the relationship between content area learning and critical thinking. Chapter 3 suggests a conceptual framework to support the information curriculum in a technological age that emphasizes processes, skills, and attitudes that apply across all disciplines—such as an attitude of inquiry, the skill of formulating questions to investigate, and the process of gathering and analyzing data. Chapter 4 links informational books to writing across the curriculum. Chapter 5 describes specific ways to use informational books in integrated themes of study.

We wish to thank our own students, both the elementary school children whom we hope will be the ultimate beneficiaries of our book and our undergraduate and graduate students. They have all been our teachers, and we are grateful each day as we learn from their ideas, questions, and concerns. They prompt us to explore new areas of inquiry and to revisit our own ideas and perspectives. We also want to thank our editor, Virginia Lanigan, and her editorial staff at Allyn and Bacon for their support during the writing of this book. We extend a very special thanks to Mary Kay Yaus at The Ohio State University at Newark, Kathy Horvath, Marjorie Glassman, and Yigal Rechtman, who all assisted in preparation of the manuscript. We thank Pam Carey for giving permission to include her web, "A House Divided," and we appreciate the suggestions for activities and learning experiences given by Sue Bauerle, Clarissa Hall, Mary Long, and Dr. Brian Edmiston. We are grateful to Dr. Bernice E. Cullinan, New York University, and to Jui-Yi Huang and Ya-Fen Lo, doctoral students at The Ohio State University who provided invaluable assistance in numerous ways. Appreciation goes also to the following reviewers for their helpful comments on the manuscript: Dr. Gail P. Silkebakken, East Central University; Dorothy J. Douglas, Monmouth College; Bonnie M. Lutz, Evansville Elementary School; and Dr. Brenda Harvey, Mount Vernon Nazarene College.

► 1

Why Use Informational Children's Books in Content Area Learning?

Imagine a dame school in colonial New England during the late 1600s. A small group of children listens to their teacher reading aloud to them from the Bible or from *Pilgrim's Progress* by John Bunyan. This scene is not so different from classrooms today in which teachers read literature aloud to their students. Currently many elementary teachers are embracing literature-based instruction, in which children's literature is used as texts for both reading and content area studies.

In this chapter we discuss reasons why informational children's books are a valuable resource in content area learning. First we share what research results have shown about the relationship between children's literature and learning. Then we describe how informational books are a distinct genre of children's literature. Next we point out some of the limitations of content area textbooks as compared with informational children's books. Lastly we discuss how informational books support an integrated curriculum.

WHAT WE KNOW ABOUT LITERATURE AND LEARNING

For more than a decade a quiet revolution has been occurring in elementary schools, as increasing numbers of teachers incorporate children's literature, not only in reading instruction, but in support of all areas of the elementary school curriculum. In 1986 Bill Honig, California's State Superintendent of Public Instruction, instituted the California Reading Initiative, which mandated the use of children's literature as the core of the reading program. A national survey conducted by Bernice Cullinan in 1989 found that many states such as Arizona, Arkansas, New York, and Hawaii were also involved in literature-based initiatives. In a study of how teachers in one state used children's literature, Scharer, Freeman, Lehman, and Allen (1993) found that 80 percent of the elementary teachers surveyed reported that their students had positive attitudes toward reading, that the teachers read aloud to their classes at least once a day, and that students had time to read a book of their own choosing daily. Reading Recovery, the highly successful program for at-risk first graders, involves children reading real books.

Research supports the benefits of using children's literature in the classroom, and the practice of teachers reading literature aloud to children has been studied extensively. Teale (1984) points out: "Virtually unquestioned by researchers is the premise that reading to children contributes directly to their early literacy development" (p. 110). Reading aloud to children shows positive links to their motivation for reading; vocabulary development; knowledge of the functions, structures, and uses of written language; general language development; and reading comprehension. Research has also indicated that the type of literature read by students influences the nature and quality of their writing (Deford, 1981; Eckhoff, 1983). In reviewing the research on the benefits of children's literature in the classroom, Galda and Cullinan (1991) conclude that "experiences with literature during the school years promote interest in reading, language development, reading achievement, and growth in writing abilities" (p. 530).

Educators and librarians advocate children's literature not only for reading programs but for use in all elementary content areas. Informational books, a genre of children's literature, can facilitate specific benefits in support of student learning across the curriculum. First, informational books encourage children to explore topics of interest and satisfy their natural curiosity. For example, answers to children's questions about the popular topic of dinosaurs can be found in such books as Kathryn Lasky's *Dinosaur Dig* (1990, Morrow) or Caroline Arnold's *Dinosaurs All Around* (1993, Clarion). Children interested in more unusual topics can satisfy their curiosity by reading books like *A Whole New Ball Game: The Story of the All-American Girls Professional Baseball League* (1993, Holt) by Sue Macy, which chronicles this professional women's baseball league from 1943–1954, or *Cookies* (1993, Macmillan) by William Jaspersohn, which takes readers inside a chocolate chip cookie factory.

Second, informational books help children see connections and interrelationships among content and concepts. When investigating the Arctic region, children learn about arctic wolves in Jim Brandenburg's *To the Top of the World: Adventures with Arctic Wolves* (1993, Walker) and arctic bears in *Polar Bear Cubs* by Downs Matthews (1989, Simon and Schuster). This initial inquiry into two popular arctic animals may lead children to find out about other plants and animals of the region described in *Land of Dark, Land of Light: The Arctic National Wildlife Refuge* by Karen Pandell (1993, Dutton). (See "Arctic Web" in Chapter 5.) Children can also link informational texts with other genres of literature to gain a more complete understanding of concepts and content. Three books about the Taino, the Native American people who welcomed Columbus, help children see connections: the powerful picture book *Encounter* (1992, Harcourt Brace) by Jane Yolen, written from the point of view of a young Taino boy; the historical novel *Morning Girl* (1992, Hyperion) by Michael Dorris, which provides a glimpse of daily Taino life from the perspectives of a brother and sister; and the informational text *The Tainos: The People Who Welcomed Columbus* (1992, Putnam) by Francine Jacobs. Children can also see connections between fictional characters with whom they empathize and the historical context in which these characters lived. In Pam Conrad's novel *Prairie Songs* (1985, HarperCollins) a minor character was a photographer, Solomon Butcher, based on an actual person. In *Prairie Visions: The Life and Times of Solomon Butcher* (1991, HarperCollins), Conrad historically portrays turn-of-the century Kansas while describing the life of Solomon Butcher and enhancing the text with Butcher's photographs.

Third, children's critical thinking and problem-solving skills are fostered as they compare and contrast books on the same topic, noting various authors' points of view, the information that is included, and the types of formats used to present the information. For instance, in recent years several children's books have been written about the 1960s civil rights movement. Children can delve into the similarities and differences among such books as Ellen Levine's *Freedom's Children: Young Civil Rights Activists Tell Their Own Stories* (1993, Putnam), James Haskins's *The March on Washington* (1993, HarperCollins), and Mildred Pitts Walter's *Mississippi Challenge* (1992, Bradbury). Children will enjoy learning more about the Negro Baseball League by comparing its presentation in *Playing America's Game: The*

Story of Negro League Baseball (1993, Lodestar) by Michael Cooper, *The Forgotten Players: The Story of Black Baseball in America* (1993, Walker) by Robert Gardner and Dennis Shortelle, and *Black Diamond: The Story of the Negro Baseball Leagues* (1994, Scholastic) by Patricia McKissack and Fredrick McKissack, Jr.

Fourth, through informational books, children learn about faraway places, past times, and new ideas and concepts. Not only do children expand and deepen their knowledge base; they stimulate their imagination as well. While few children may have visited Asia, they can experience a young girl's daily life in modern Korea in *Chi-Hoon, A Korean Girl* (1993, Boyds Mills Press) by Patricia McMahon. They cannot travel back in time, but the lives of children in earlier times are revealed in *Hiding to Survive: Stories of Jewish Children Rescued from the Holocaust* (1994, Clarion) by Maxine Rosenberg, a book about World War II; and *Children of the Dust Bowl* (1992, Crown) by Jerry Stanley about children's lives during the Depression in California.

Finally, informational books help children inquire and problem solve as their reading leads them to question and investigate. They will appreciate scientists' inquiry stance and recognize that we still have much to learn about elusive creatures while reading *The News about Dinosaurs* (1989, Bradbury) by Patricia Lauber. What fun children will have participating in the amazing science activities in *Wanna Bet? Science Challenges to Fool You* (1993, Lothrop, Lee & Shepard) by Vicki Cobb and Kathy Darling. Or they will marvel at how scientists have gained insights and information about Antarctica in Laurence Pringle's *Antarctica: The Last Unspoiled Continent* (1992, Simon and Schuster).

Educators have pointed out the specific value of informational books in content area learning and described their benefits to the social studies (Bosma, 1992; Person and

Cullinan, 1992; Beck and McKeown, 1991; Carter and Abrahamson, 1993) and to science (Bosma, 1992; Frank, 1992; Lapp and Flood, 1993). History comes alive as children identify with real people and events. For example, Milton Meltzer (1993), well known for his informative historical books that rely on original source materials that "let people speak in their own words" (p. 28), points out that "when young people read this kind of history—original documents left behind by the people of the time...—they are helped to locate their individual lives in the chain of generations" (p. 29). Informational books in social studies cover a wide range of areas such as geography, history, government, multicultural understanding, and contemporary issues.

Informational books benefit science instruction as well. Nordstrom (1992) indicates that science trade books "can support the inquiry approach to science...a nonfiction book offers an opportunity to transform a child's interest in a subject to knowledge about it" (p. 59). Crook and Lehman (1990) observe that "trade books are diverse in subject matter and depth of coverage and are appropriate for a wide range of reading abilities. These books communicate a sense of wonder that attracts children again and again" (p. 22).

Links between informational books and mathematics are also being generated (Bosma, 1992; Cohn and Wendt, 1993; Whitin and Wilde, 1992). Whitin and Wilde (1992) in *Read Any Good Math Lately?* advocate using children's literature to teach mathematics because it shows how mathematics is essential in everyone's daily life, thereby providing a way to contextualize math as well as portray it as a part of the human experience. Further, literature "celebrates mathematics as a language" (p. 5) and "addresses humanistic, affective elements of mathematics" (p. 9). Children's literature can enhance specific math concepts and reinforce problem-solving strategies.

Graphics that clarify and extend the text are another reason for the use of informational books in content learning. Photographs, paintings, drawings, original documents, maps, charts, graphs, and reproductions of artwork are the kinds of graphics that spark readers' interest. When concepts are abstract or outside readers' prior knowledge and experience, illustrations give them the visual representation needed to understand the text.

EXPOSITORY TEXT

Informational books represent the genre of literature whose primary purpose is to inform. Authors of informational books employ an expository writing style that has characteristics different from narrative style. Researchers have looked at how children develop in their ability to comprehend and produce expository text and have delineated the unique features of expository text structure. But the strict lines between exposition and narrative are beginning to blur. As Rosenblatt (1991) points out, "narrative (story) is found not only in novels but also in scientific accounts of geological change or historical accounts of political events or social life" (p. 444). Writers of informational books for children often adopt a narrative framework for their work. Award-winning children's writer Russell Freedman believes that "the task of the nonfiction writer is to find the story—the narrative line—that exists in nearly every subject" (1992, p. 3). Conversely, many works of fiction certainly convey information about people, places, events, and ideas.

Relationship to Children's Literacy Development

Theory and research on children's literacy development have focused almost exclusively on narrative. A commonly held belief that "narrative is primary" exists in the study of chil-

dren's development of literacy. Scholarly work has emphasized the value of story in reading, writing, and oral language development. Many educators espouse narrative as
the natural mode of expression and say that exposition is
more difficult for young children to read and write. Pappas
(1991) calls this emphasis into question and points out that
little research has been conducted on young children's reading and writing of nonstory genres. Hiebert (1991) concurs,
believing that "expository text should consume a substantial
part of the elementary literacy and language curriculum" (p.
482). When children reach fourth grade, they are asked to
engage in more reading of content area textbooks, and it is
at this time, often referred to as "fourth-grade slump," that
many students experience reading difficulty. Beck and
McKeown (1991) offer several possible explanations for the
difficulty students seem to experience with content area
texts: unfamiliarity with expository text, unfamiliarity with
the content, poor organization of the content.

In recent years, researchers have begun to look at how
young children relate to expository text. Langer (1986)
points out: "Common sense tells us that young children
share information all the time—and that this should provide
the use-driven basis for their later encounters with exposition in written form" (p. 32). Newkirk (1989) provides an
analysis of specific types of nonnarrative writing done by
young children (labeling of pictures, lists, persuasive writing, and letters) and concludes that young children demonstrate competence in a range of writing genres including
those that demand analysis, explanation, and argument.
Bissex (1980) found that her son's writing between the ages
of 5 and 9 was primarily informational. Christie (1987) challenges the view that children learn to write narratives first
and points out that in Australian schools, children's first
writing attempts are observation and recounts, both of which

are factual, not narrative. Christie further argues that "young children write what they are enabled to write...they have no necessary predisposition to create narratives or any other forms, and they will seek to produce those forms which opportunity has allowed them to learn" (p. 208). In a study of kindergarten children's repeated pretend readings of both expository and narrative books, Pappas (1993) found that children were equally successful in their reenactments regardless of genre.

Research focusing on upper elementary and high school students' comprehension and production of expository text has indicated that a positive relationship exists between students' understanding of expository text structure and comprehension scores. In a summary of research on text structure instruction for expository text, Pearson and Fielding (1991) conclude that

> any sort of systematic attention to clues that reveal how authors attempt to relate ideas to one another or any sort of systematic attempt to impose structure upon a text, especially in some sort of visual rerepresentation of the relationships among key ideas, facilitates comprehension as well as both short-term and long-term memory for the text" (p. 832).

In addition, instruction in expository text structure has a positive effect on students' writing of expository text. (Raphael, Englert, and Kirschner, 1989)

In a study of third and fifth graders' expository writing, Cox, Shanahan, and Tinzmann (1991) discussed with children what they knew about a specified topic before the children read an article on that topic. The children further discussed the article and then wrote a report on the topic for a group of children their own age. Results indicated that the children definitely understood the function of exposition, as well as their audience. The authors suggest that "it would seem wise to provide children with substantial opportunities to read and use a variety of well written expository texts" (p. 207).

Structure

Narrative writing has a basic story structure, often termed story grammar. Story grammar includes the setting, characters, problem faced by the main character, episodes in resolving the problem, and a resolution. A central theme binds the story together. Expository text also has structure that can be described. What are the characteristics of expository text that distinguish it from narrative? Kent (1984) describes four such differences. While narrative is usually written in the first or third person, expository text does not necessarily indicate a person reference. Narrative is based on the action of characters, while expository text is driven more by the content being explained. Narrative is generally written in the past tense or historical present, while expository text uses various tenses. Narrative is most frequently organized by chronology, while expository text may be connected in numerous ways.

Irwin and Baker (1989) identify six types of organizational patterns for arranging and connecting ideas typically found in expository text. One pattern, description, describes the subject or topic, perhaps by listing characteristics. An example of this pattern can be found in Seymour Simon's *Wolves* (1993, HarperCollins): "A wolf might be almost any color, from white to black, through shades and mixtures of cream, gray, brown, and red" (u.p.).

A second pattern, temporal sequence, presents events in the order in which they happen. Authors may use key words such as *next, first, then, finally, before* in using this pattern. *A River Ran Wild* (1992, Harcourt Brace) by Lynne Cherry is organized temporally as the history of the Nashua River is recounted. Phrases indicating the passage of time introduce sentences, such as "at the start of the new century" or "the next morning."

A third pattern, explanation, provides causes, effects, or reasons for various phenonema and events. A reader may find words like *because, so, thus, consequently, as a result of* when this pattern is used. For example, in Milton Meltzer's *The Amazing Potato* (1992, HarperCollins) he explains that when the native peoples of Peru migrated to the Andes, "the food they were used to eating—manioc and maize—would not grow on mountains lofting miles into the cold skies. So these immigrants had to find other vegetables to eat" (p. 9).

In the fourth pattern, comparison/contrast, two events, concepts, or phenomena are compared and contrasted. Key words in this pattern are *by comparison, similarly, but, on the other hand, unlike.* In the book *What's the Difference? A Guide to Some Familiar Animal Look-Alikes* (1993, Clarion) Elizabeth Lacey compares and contrasts similar animals and describes the distinction between a buffalo and bison: "Buffalo are externally different from bison and internally different as well—bison have 14 pairs of ribs, buffalo have 13" (p. 13).

A fifth pattern is to define or give examples by using words like *for example, such as, to illustrate,* and *namely.* Bruce Brooks discusses the six senses of animals in *Making Sense: Animal Perception and Communication* (1993, Farrar Straus Giroux) and writes, "So, given the fact that birds, for example, have better sight and better voices than we do..." (p. 6).

In the sixth pattern, problem/solution, the author identifies a problem and its causes, then delineates a solution or solutions. *Come Back, Salmon* (1992, Sierra Club Books) by Molly Cone is a good example of this pattern as children at Jackson

Elementary ponder the problem of "where did all the salmon go?" and find ways to bring the salmon back to Pigeon Creek.

LIMITATIONS OF CONTENT AREA TEXTS

Textbooks are the dominant form of instructional materials in the elementary curriculum—some would even claim that they have become the national curricula (Woodward and Elliott, 1990). While textbooks have consistently caused controversy and criticism, the attacks on them have intensified over the past decade. In *A Nation at Risk: The Imperative for Educational Reform* (1983), textbooks were specifically targeted for improvement: "Textbooks and other tools of learning and teaching should be upgraded and updated to assure more rigorous content" (p. 28). In her analysis of textbooks for the Council for Basic Education, Tyson-Bernstein (1988) summarized the common textbook concerns: "Publishers and editors create textbooks that confuse students with non-sequitors, mislead them with misinformation, bore them with pointlessly arid writing" (p. 3). Research since the publication of *A Nation at Risk* has focused on three specific areas of textbook weakness: reading difficulty, content, and quality of writing.

Reading Difficulty

Textbooks have simultaneously been criticized for being both too easy and too difficult. The use of readability formulas has been blamed for the "dumbing down" of texts. Overreliance on a computed readability formula has actually caused texts to become more difficult rather than easier to understand (Bernstein, 1985). In a comprehensive study of the reading difficulty of texts, Chall and Conrad (1991) found that fourth-grade textbooks in both science and social studies were above the reading levels of the majority of children using them. Science texts were generally more difficult than social studies texts. They concluded that the texts "represented a narrow range of difficulty for each grade we analyzed, more narrow than the range of reading ability found among students" (p. 111).

Similarly, Wood and Wood (1988) in an analysis of fourth-grade science textbooks found they were too difficult for fourth-graders who were reading at grade level. Further, for students reading in the lower quarter and for low socio-economic status students reading at grade level, seven of the ten texts studied were too difficult to comprehend. Woodward, Elliott and Nagel (1986) feel that the use of readability formulas has caused "short sentences, simple vocabulary and the exclusion of connectors and referents that help make text easier for youngsters to comprehend" (p. 52). Sewall (1988a) also bemoans readability formulas that have led publishers to "break up complex sentences, shorten paragraphs, and excise stylistic flourishes. The conjunctions, modifiers, and clauses that help create subtle connections and advance student understanding are routinely cut" (p. 555). In addition, Woodward and Elliott (1990) point out that science texts introduce an overwhelming number of new, unfamiliar, and highly specialized terms.

Therefore, science and social studies textbooks generally appear to be too difficult for the majority of students reading them. In addition, they do not provide for the wide range of reading abilities usually found in an elementary classroom.

Content

Concerns regarding textbooks have also dealt with the inclusion of too much information on the one hand and the hesitation to include "controversial" subject matter on the other.

Textbook publishers feel pressure from many sources, such as state education agencies, and they attempt to make their products be all things to all people. As Tyson-Bernstein (1988) points out, textbooks "cover more information than can be treated respectfully" (p. 9). Textbooks in science and social studies suffer from what is referred to as the "mentioning" problem. Names, dates, terms, facts are mentioned but very little is discussed in depth with vignettes, examples, or adequate discussion of big ideas and concepts. This superficial, disconnected treatment often leaves students confused and unable to understand the content (Tyson-Bernstein, 1988; Woodward, Elliott, and Nagel, 1986).

On the other hand, omission of important content is another concern raised (Tyson-Bernstein, 1988). Sewall (1988a) points out that "incandescent acts of charity and wisdom, triumphs of technology, the exploits of heroes and villains are all disappearing from textbooks" (p. 556). Textbook publishers avoid controversial topics, resulting in a lack of meaningful and authentic coverage of such areas as evolution, religion, and the representation of women and minorities.

Textbooks have also been criticized for inaccurate content. In a study of how elementary science textbooks discuss magnetism, Barrow (1990) discovered that some science texts identify the location of the magnet's poles at the end of the magnet. Barrow points out that "this could promote misconception because a ceramic magnet's pole is not at the end of the magnet, but located on surfaces" (p. 719). Another concern with content is that textbooks assume students have sufficient background knowledge to comprehend the new material being presented. An analysis of social studies textbooks by Beck and McKeown (1991) found that "many ideas and events portrayed in the books were beyond a young student's grasp because the texts assumed unrealistic levels of knowledge" (p. 484). Finally, elementary content textbooks emphasize facts to be memorized rather than conceptual development, problem-solving, or higher-order thinking skills.

Quality of Writing

Textbooks have been criticized for poor writing that is "choppy, stilted and monotonous" (Tyson-Bernstein, 1988, p. 21). In a study of the literary quality of American history textbooks at grades 5, 8, and 11, Sewall (1988b) reported results of reviewing three popular fifth-grade elementary social studies texts. He concludes: "The prose style of most textbooks is bland and voiceless, excessive coverage makes textbooks boring, textbook format and graphics diminish the style and coherence of the running text" (p. 35). Britton, Gulgoz, and Glynn (1993) suggest three explanations for poor writing in textbooks: The textbook author may not be a good writer, the author's subject matter expertise may interfere with clear writing, and restrictions placed on textbook authors (e.g., certain topics, readability formulas) may impede effective writing. Textbook writing has often been described as "inconsiderate" in contrast to "considerate" writing that arranges and connects ideas logically, avoids including irrelevant information, and considers the readers' prior knowledge (Meyer, 1991).

Several educators have noted that science texts lack clear explanations of phenomena and well-written, rich descriptions (Finley, 1991; Holliday, 1991). Beck and McKeown (1991) similarly found elementary social studies texts lacking coherence and providing inadequate explanations. A study by Beck, McKeown, and Gromell (1989) examined elementary social studies textbooks and determined that the sequence in which information is presented often lacks coherence and that unfamiliar language is used.

Overcoming Textbook Limitations with Informational Books

Children's informational books support content area learning and provide a supplement to or a substitute for the traditional textbook. These books address the concerns leveled against texts: They delve into a subject in more depth, they are written in an engaging and interesting style, and new information is introduced in a meaningful context. The concern regarding text difficulty can be overcome by using informational books. Many books written at various reading levels are available on topics generally found in the elementary curriculum such as dinosaurs, ecology, animals, Native Americans, and transportation. Further, as Beck and McKeown (1991) point out, trade books can provide multiple perspectives about the subject being studied rather than the textbook's single perspective. In addition, an informational book's format and graphics provide clarity and extend content. By comparing material on the same subject in an elementary textbook and an informational children's book, we can see these differences.

Take for example how a fourth-grade science text deals with the topic of protective coloration. As part of a subsection on "Adaptations for Protection," two paragraphs are dedicated to the discussion of protective coloration. They read as follows:

> Many animals hide from their predators. They are adapted to look like their surroundings. The shape of some animals helps them hide. Notice the insect in the picture on the left. This katydid looks like a leaf. How does looking like a leaf help protect this insect from being eaten?
>
> The colors or patterns of some animals help protect them. This **protective coloration** helps the animals hide from their predators. Find the flounder in the pic-

ture. It spends most of its life on the ocean floor. The colors of its upper side change to match the background of its surroundings. What the flounder looks like helps it escape being eaten. The flounder's behavior also is an adaptation. The flounder lies very still and blends into its background. (*Discover Science,* Scott, Foresman, 1991, p. 94)

It is interesting to note in this passage that the term *camouflage* is never mentioned. Instead, the phrase *protective coloration* is used. In contrast, the entire book *Hiding Out: Camouflage in the Wild* by James Martin (1993, Crown) deals with how animals protect themselves through camouflage. Because interesting, specific examples supported with color photographs are discussed, the term *camouflage* would be clearly understood by fourth-grade children. One page from the book highlights the difference in writing and content in this informational science book in contrast to the textbook.

The orchid mantis is a master of camouflage—the art of hiding while in plain sight. Camouflage enables predators like the orchid mantis to hide while they lie in wait for their prey. For other animals, camouflage is a method of protection from their enemies.

Animals blend into the background in several ways. Their colors and patterns may match their surroundings. The shape of their bodies may resemble some other object, such as a stick, a leaf, or a flower. Crests and frills may break up the outline of bodies, disguising their real shape and fooling the eye. They may even behave like something else—a fluttering leaf or a dangerous animal, for example. (p. 4)

The difference in content and writing between textbooks and informational children's books can also be seen in social studies textbooks. In a fourth-grade Houghton Mifflin social studies textbook (1991) a short section headed "Hunters on the Plains" describes the native Sioux tribe. The relationship of the buffalo to the Sioux culture is explained as follows:

> The huge herds of buffalo that fed on the grasses of the plains were the most important resource for the Sioux. The Sioux's whole culture was based on the buffalo. ...Each Sioux family lived in a buffalo-skin tent called a tipi (TEE pee). The Sioux people dressed in buffalo skins, and ate buffalo meat. Horns and bones from the animal were made into tools and weapons such as spoons and spearheads. Products made from buffalo and other plains animals supplied the Sioux with most of their daily needs. (pp. 155–156)

This paragraph can be compared to the discussion of the buffalo's relationship to the Sioux in *The Sioux* (1993, Holiday House) by Virginia Driving Hawk Sneve, herself a Sioux.

> On the Plains, the buffalo was the center of Sioux life. The men hunted and killed the buffalo and gave it to the women, who butchered it, wasting nothing. They made tipis, beds, blankets, moccasins, clothing, and robes from the hides. They made storage boxes from strong rawhide and used leather strips to lace the tipis together and to make bridles. Buffalo bones were used to make tools for farming, scraping, and sewing. In the winter the ribs were used as sleds.
>
> The buffalo was also the main food source of the Sioux. The women cooked the meat in a bowl they made by stretching the buffalo's stomach over a wooden frame. They filled the bowl with water that they heated with hot stones. The women dried the meat to eat in the winter. A favorite dish was *wasna* or pemmican. It was made by pounding dried meat and berries into fine bits and mixing them with suet. The Indians ate this tasty, nutritious food when the village moved or when the men went on a hunting trip.
>
> The buffalo made the Sioux wealthy. After the white men came, the Sioux traded buffalo hides and beaver

pelts for guns, iron kettles, calico, beads, and whiskey, thus becoming even wealthier. (pp. 9–10)

The tone of the textbook presentation is one of neutrality toward the topic, while the informational book's tone conveys respect for the Sioux and their culture. Further, the informational book provides more detail and description than the text and also portrays the value of the buffalo to the Sioux way of life. Color illustrations by award-winning illustrator Ronald Himler support and extend the written description.

THE INTEGRATED CURRICULUM

In recent years, educators at all levels have advocated an integrated curriculum that emphasizes the connections among subject areas. In the real world outside of school we don't compartmentalize our thinking as math, science, and social studies. Instead, we apply the content, skills, and processes we have learned to think about, discuss and solve real-life problems and situations. In thinking about topics of high interest to students, such as the environment, space travel and the solar system, and homelessness, natural links occur across all curricular areas incorporating language arts and children's literature.

As with many "buzzwords" in education, different conceptions of an integrated curriculum abound. In language arts, teachers emphasize the integration of reading, writing, listening, speaking, and thinking or keeping language "whole." Oral and written language form an integrated web that cannot be separated into discrete, isolated parts. When we enter into conversation, we speak and listen. When we write, we read what we have written. Research supports the relationship of oral language to literacy, the connections between reading and writing, and the integrated way that children develop oral and written language.

Another view of the integrated curriculum advocates language arts across the curriculum, or the inclusion of reading, writing, and oral language activities in content area learning. The National Council of Teachers of English pamphlet "Learning Through Language" (1993) calls for action in all disciplines to create classrooms where "language is used for learning...places where students talk, read, and write frequently, places where they learn better and their learning lasts longer."

Others emphasize integration in the content of science, social studies, and other subjects to foster connections around big concepts and ideas. Peetom (1993) eloquently summarizes current thinking about integration:

> First, a classroom ought to be integrated, because life is integrated. ...[c]hildren so experience life in an integrated way that it will take more than a few weeks in school benches to knock this good stuff out of them. Children have no trouble jumping from one interest to another within a theme, and often with a quicksilver logic that we adults can discover and delight in. As we look at the learning of little children to discover what learning is really like, we discover that learning is seeing connection. (p. 7)

A 1991 themed issue of *Educational Leadership* elaborates many approaches to integration. Fogarty (1991) describes ten distinct models for integrating the curriculum, which she arranges along a continuum from models within single disciplines, then across several disciplines, to the continuum's far end with models integrating within and across learners. Yet the concept of an integrated curriculum is hardly new. John Dewey and the progressive educators advocated child-centered education that emphasized an experiential curriculum based on students' interests stressing connections with life experiences, and rebelling against the artificial distinctions of discrete subject matter. In his classic work *Experience and Education,* Dewey (1938) discussed how subject matter cannot be separated from experience. He asserted: "It is a sound educational principle that students should be introduced to scientific subject-matter and be initiated into its facts and laws through acquaintance with everyday social applications" (p. 80).

As early as the 1880s, Col. Francis W. Parker, as principal of the Cook County Normal School in Chicago and then as superintendent of schools in Quincy, Massachusetts, encouraged the use of a "core curriculum." The core curriculum concept stressed that curriculum should not be organized into separate subjects like reading, grammar, and arithmetic but rather should be organized around a unifying core of studies that related the various subject matters. Core curriculum advocates of the 1940s and 1950s also reacted against a subject matter curriculum and affirmed curriculum based on students' needs and interests. Its proponents believed traditional subjects should be replaced by "units of life experiences," "centers of interest," "problem area studies," or "social living themes" such as "Protecting Life and Health" or "Living in the Neighborhood" (Edwards and Richey, 1963).

In the 1960s and 1970s the English "infant school" (schools for children ages 5 to 7) and the "open classroom" in the United States included an integrated curriculum. In an integrated curriculum a theme, concept, book, or problem provides the focus for a variety of learning experiences that encompass several subject areas. This approach gives the curriculum a more unified and cohesive base, enabling students to make connections and to more easily perceive and understand relationships. In 1967 the Plowden Report, which supported informal education in English infant schools, described the importance of building curriculum based on children's interests and devalued rigid distinctions among subject matter. It recommended organizing curriculum around a topic that "cuts across the boundaries of subjects and is treated as its nature requires without reference to subjects as such" (Silberman, 1973, p. 507).

The English infant school and open classroom also provided flexible scheduling throughout the day, which came to be known as the "integrated day." Students were actively engaged in learning unconstrained by demarcations of time for specific subjects. Perrone (1972) explains that teachers in "open education" were

> organizing ways to explore the more integrative qualities of knowledge, skills, appreciation, and understanding, rather than maintaining the divisions of knowledge and skills into various kinds of subject matter, that is, reading, mathematics, social studies, science, music, and art. They see integration of learning, its wholeness, as an essential base for personalizing the educational process. (p. 8)

One popular approach to an integrated curriculum among elementary teachers today is "theme teaching." A theme of study gives children opportunities to explore a topic in an interconnected way. Conceptual development is encouraged as children examine the theme's interrelated elements in natural and meaningful learning experiences. Student inquiry, active participation, and higher-level thinking are essential. Reading, writing, and oral language are woven throughout the learning experiences, with children's literature used to support the content and concepts being developed. For instance, if students wished to explore the theme of the "Rain Forest," they might consider such related topics as plant life, animal life, location of rain forests, climate of rain forests, people and cultures, and the future of rain forests. The children could consult informational books such as *Nature's Green Umbrella* (1994, Morrow) by Gail Gibbons, *Antonio's Rain Forest* (1993, Carolrhoda Books) by

Anna Lewington, and *Why Save the Rain Forest?* (1993, Messner) by Donald Silver as they investigate rain forest topics and engage in math activities to create maps using scale, compute various statistics regarding plants and animals, or graph rain forest temperature during different seasons. Students might write journal entries about ecological efforts, riddles about jungle animals, an *ABC* book of jungle plants, a news article on ways to save the rain forest, or a descriptive poem about the rain forest.

Several educators propose science as the core for an integrated curriculum. Mechling and Kepler (1991) point out similarities between science process skills and those in language arts/reading, math, and social studies. For example, in all these subjects, students predict, classify, compare and contrast, collect data or take notes, and analyze and interpret data. Cohen and Staley (1982) recognize the potential of science to foster children's critical-thinking skills and to serve as a natural basis for reading, oral language, and writing activities.

New curriculum projects focus on integration. The Mid-California Science Improvement Program involves elementary teachers in designing a year-long theme with major monthly components that make "science the ingredient that unites all other subjects" (Greene, 1991, p. 43). Themes such as "The World Beneath My Feet," "Keeper of the Earth," and "California, the Edge" engage students in reading, writing, problem solving, computing, measuring, and expressing themselves artistically as they work in groups to explore the theme. A math curriculum project for grades 4–6, *My Travels with Gulliver,* includes literature, writing, and art. Funded by the National Science Foundation, this curriculum uses excerpts from *Gulliver's Travels* and an original short story as a basis for mathematical problem solving, writing, drawing, and discussing (Kleiman, 1991).

Children's books have an important role to play in an integrated curriculum. Informational books can be read aloud by the teacher or independently by students. Students consult them for reference as they seek answers to questions and investigate topics. Informational books are effective models for students' own writing across the curriculum (Freeman, 1991; Salesi, 1992). As informational books are incorporated by teachers into integrated curricula, content area educators are developing standards for their disciplines that include specific attention to language and literacy. In the next chapter we shall discuss recent curriculum standards in science, math, and social studies that emphasize conceptual learning and integration, rather than learning facts in isolation or fragmenting content. These standards promote the application of discipline knowledge to real-world problems and situations. Literacy is embedded in each of these standards as language is used to develop knowledge, connections, and applications.

▶ 2

Current Trends in Content Area Curriculum

Every day we pick up the newspaper or other publication to be confronted with a story about the academic failings of America's students. They trail students in other industrialized countries in math and science skills, they have difficulty locating places on a map, and they have little sense of history (Hammack, 1990; Ravitch and Finn, 1987).

Much of the blame for their poor academic achievement is attributed to current teaching methods emphasizing direct instruction and rote learning, the writing style used in classroom textbooks, and curriculum materials that are essentially irrelevant to knowledge that will be needed in the twenty-first century (Saul and Jagusch, 1991). To counteract this situation, various teaching associations, state legislatures, and federal study commissions have proposed the development of standards for each of the content areas. The intention is to implement the standards on a national level; they would apply to teaching practices, curriculum content, assessment practices, and student achievement. Standards in mathematics were developed and adopted by the National Council of Teachers of Mathematics in 1989; standards for the science and social studies content areas have recently been formulated and published by their respective professional associations.

In defense of content area standards the argument is tendered that practical applications in these disciplines are not taught, nor are the subjects integrated for a comprehensive view of how each one is vital to an understanding of the other. Science should not be taught as a separate subject but should be integrated with math, social studies, and technology, which can be accomplished with greater emphasis on problem-solving and critical-thinking skills (NCTM, 1989; Rutherford and Ahlgren, 1990). Too much irrelevant detail is taught so that students lose sight of the way math and science connect with each other and with the new technological systems now used in business and technology (NCTM, 1989).

Further, there is little agreement about what should be taught. It is no longer necessary to have students memorize multiplication or chemical element tables. Instead, each standard proposes that students should engage in hands-on learning activities, such as proposing and testing theorems that lead to improved problem-solving and comprehension skills. Emphasis has been on teaching outcomes and products, but the standards for mathematics, science, and social studies now propose emphasizing the processes and comprehension of their content areas. Such an effort would require retraining teachers to teach the revised content curricula, using media more relevant to students' expectations of text, modernizing school laboratories, and updating technological equipment.

Criticism has been leveled at several areas of math, science, and social studies teaching methods and curricula. The most often heard criticism is directed against textbooks, charging they encourage rote memorization of answers rather than an attitude of scientific inquiry, questioning, exploration of the material, and critical thinking. Too often content area textbooks fail to adequately explain key concepts, and they use vocabulary that is too technical for elementary students (Armbruster, 1984; National Research Council, 1990).

Another frequently heard criticism is that teachers are often unprepared to teach elementary science and math courses, having limited knowledge of these disciplines themselves (Rutherford and Ahlgren, 1990). Many elementary school teachers, as well as many at the junior and senior high level, do not have the requisite undergraduate coursework to adequately teach mathematics, science, or social studies courses, and rely too heavily on "teachers' editions" of textbooks, failing to encourage students to work together collaboratively in a spirit of scientific inquiry.

Another shortcoming of elementary school content area curricula occurs with the effort to be all-inclusive rather than to teach only what is essential to achieve scientific literacy. As new information has become available over the past decades, it has been grafted onto existing curricula without any distinction about what learning will be necessary to compete in the global village of the twenty-first century. Rutherford and Ahlgren (1990) and the committee members of the National Council of Teachers of Mathematics (1989) agree that existing content curricula place too much emphasis on drilling of mindless details and memorization skills and too little focus on the essential nature of their subjects; and that schools do not have to teach more of these subjects but, rather, need to streamline the curriculum and teach only what will be essential in the future. The lessons of science, math, and social studies, it is argued, must contribute to students' abilities to participate as socially responsible citizens, able to see issues from a historical perspective and to make decisions based on sound judgment. Educators in all three disciplines charge that schools fail to do this as their curricula are presently structured.

The elementary level mathematics curriculum is challenged by members of the National Council of Teachers of Mathematics as having the same shortcomings as the elementary science curriculum. The council, through its Commission on Standards for School Mathematics (1989), writes that for too long what has been taught and the method of teaching have emphasized rote knowledge, memorization, and computational skills. Such a narrow vision of what constitutes mathematical competence hampers the development of higher-order thinking skills such as problem-solving and reasoning abilities and fails to encourage the development of insights about the nature of mathematics. In such an atmosphere, the commission writes (NCTM, 1989), mathematics ceases to be a meaning-making experience and becomes a series of task-oriented skills that emphasize finding the right answers. Instead of becoming active participants in the mathematics problem-solving process, students learn to become passive memorizers of number skills. Looking to the future, the committee notes that higher-order mathematics, language, and thinking skills will be needed for success in the workplace and that workers will need to read and understand instructions in order to manipulate advanced technologies in the next century. A new process-oriented curriculum emphasizing critical reading skills can help achieve this goal.

In social studies education a similar pattern of criticism emerges. Here, too, the culprits are seen as poorly written textbooks that do not encourage an understanding of the major concepts being taught or the enhancement of critical-thinking skills and the inability of students to draw on background knowledge to comprehend expository text. Beck, McKeown, and Gromoll (1989) note that students' lack of background knowledge in the subject compounds their difficulty in interpreting unfamiliar expository text, especially when a coherent writing style is absent. This criticism also applies to texts in other content areas. Beck and colleagues (1989) note that when ideas and events are presented in textbooks, an unrealistic assumption is made that elementary students are already familiar with the facts and events and that no background substantiation is needed.

Textbooks do not create a sense of the time they are depicting but seem to teach facts in isolation. Science and mathematics texts do not portray the excitement of great discoveries and the impetus such discoveries give to other scientists, encouraging them to continue their labors. Social studies textbooks do not transmit the flavor of an era or demonstrate the impact of literature, art, science, and architecture upon political ideologies of an era. Nor is the impact of philosophical movements and major events on people and governments adequately presented. Many educators (Levstik, 1990; Ravitch and Finn, 1987) propose including narrative text, journals, diaries, speeches, essays, and other original sources as standard curriculum materials.

SCIENCE—THEORETICAL UNDERPINNINGS AND CURRICULUM INNOVATIONS

The learning theories cited by the mathematics, science, and social studies disciplines are consistent with current theories about children's cognitive development and how they learn to be effective readers. Emphasis is placed on making their learning an active, hands-on practice, with students reflecting on their own learning outcomes and monitoring their critical reading processes. It is constantly noted that students must be prepared for a workplace that will require them to keep pace with the introduction of new technology and with seeking new careers or job training. They must, as students and workers, be able to adapt to new situations, assimilate new information, and solve problems adeptly, all of which requisites are also crucial to successful reading programs. The recommendations of each content area committee for achieving discipline literacy appear to be innovative but, in fact, are consistent with current theory based on research in reading and elementary education.

Defining Scientific Literacy

Scientific literacy reflects a historical point of view that emphasizes the interconnectedness of the physical, biological, psychological, and social worlds. It encourages a distinct way of observing, thinking about, experimenting with, and validating phenomena in all of the scientific disciplines. The American Association for the Advancement of Science (Rutherford and Ahlgren, 1990) offers a definition of scientific literacy that emphasizes quality and depth of understanding of scientific processes rather than the traditional breadth of coverage emphasizing memorization of pre-determined facts.

Scientific literacy encompasses

> being familiar with the natural world and respecting its unity; being aware of some of the important ways in which mathematics, technology, and the sciences depend upon one another; understanding some of the key concepts and principles of science; having a capacity for scientific ways of thinking; knowing that science, mathematics, and technology are human enterprises, and knowing what that implies about their strengths and limitations; and being able to use scientific knowledge and ways of thinking for personal and social purposes. (Rutherford and Ahlgren, 1990, p. x)

Simply put, scientific literacy implies the ability to apply scientific concepts and knowledge to all aspects of life, from simple, everyday matters to understanding and solving the most complex problems affecting the universe.

Science Standards

The American Association for the Advancement of Science recommends that the science curriculum be taught within the context of its relevance for the individual and society (Rutherford and Ahlgren, 1990). The recommendations emphasize that students need to understand how science coordinates with real-life themes related to political and cultural issues and how it impacts decisions about the environment, health care, and the economy.

The standards (National Research Council, 1994) also propose that students learn the history of science, its evolution, and how society has struggled to control the environment and human destiny through scientific endeavors. Such a perspective will, in turn, lead to an understanding of the effect of new technologies on society and how the different branches of science, mathematics, and social studies meld together as new technologies emerge, developed for use in the workplace, laboratory, and home.

The wide-ranging reforms recommended for kindergarten through high school content curricula and for teaching methodologies require equally sweeping changes in the undergraduate and graduate preparation of teachers, the availability of up-to-date technologies in all school districts, the introduction of new textbooks that emphasize understanding concepts and reasoning skills over memorization, and changes in student assessment methodologies. Implementing these changes requires careful planning, which the standards for each content area are intended to foster.

The standards present a common core of learning for students at all ability levels from kindergarten through twelfth grade. All students, by design, should be able to understand basic concepts embedded in the standards. In response to society's need for a highly sophisticated, technologically informed citizenry, the standards are intended for every student, regardless of gender, race, ethnicity, national origin, socio-economic background, or physical disability.

Practices intended to convey fundamental understandings in the natural sciences curriculum are recommended for three areas believed to be most significant for school-age youngsters: the physical sciences, life sciences, and earth and space sciences (National Research Council, 1994). In each of these domains, students in the elementary grades should be given opportunities to learn from direct, hands-on experiences with the familiar world around them. They should be encouraged to observe, describe, and manipulate this world as they learn what scientists really do in their laboratories and in the field. The excitement of scientific exploration and discovery has to be made evident to children. As they are written, the standards require that textbooks and other educational materials project an accurate model of scientific inquiry by reflecting the demand for evidence and deductive reasoning that working scientists demand of themselves. Science should not be presented as a remote, sterile discipline far removed from real-life situations but, rather, as an opportunity for hands-on activity that has relevance for children's lives (National Research Council, 1994).

Instead of burdening the curriculum with more and more "facts" as new scientific data are learned, the standards committee (National Research Council, 1994) recommends selecting scientific information that is currently highly significant and which will be essential to know in the future and concentrating on teaching that. In this way, fewer facts have to be memorized and students can concentrate on learning concepts that can be reinforced and expanded in succeeding grades as their ability to absorb new ideas matures (Rutherford and Ahlgren, 1990; National Research Council, 1994).

It is recommended that topics proposed in the new standards, such as the characteristics of and changes in objects and materials, be taught in a developmentally appropriate manner. In grades K–4 children learn best by observing, manipulating, and classifying objects. The new curriculum would give them many opportunities to do this and reflect on their observations, accompanied, perhaps, by the students' own illustrations or simple one- or two-word descriptions (Halliday, 1975; Ryan and Ellis, 1974).

As they move into the middle grades, students will be expected to use their primary grade experiences and continue to investigate the properties of objects, study their characteristics, and create models to clarify their explanations. They will be expected to make accurate measurements, design and conduct appropriate experiments, and use correct terminology and quantitative descriptions. As they continue studying the physical sciences in high school, students should be able to investigate, describe, explain, and predict the structure and reactions of simple compounds and be able to make reasonable decisions about similar processes (National Research Council, 1994).

In presenting science learning as an inquiry-based discipline, the science standards emphasize helping children understand how the principles of scientific inquiry operate. Children will learn science the way scientists learn: through asking questions about their world, through making observations, through inquiring and investigating phenomena. Learning this way requires a new focus in the curriculum and in teaching that is much closer to a philosophy of using trade books in the classroom than it is to a traditional reliance on textbooks. In inquiry-based learning a hands-on approach is used along with emphasis on critical-thinking skills. In this way, students come to an understanding of the intended science concepts and the way scientists conduct inquiries and investigations.

How does all this relate to reading and the use of trade books in content area teaching? The standards do not recommend cramming more data and facts into the science curriculum but, rather, teaching essential scientific knowledge more effectively. Science textbooks are criticized for stressing correct answers rather than encouraging exploration and discussion of concepts and memorizing bits of information rather than using critical-thinking skills to understand ideas in context. Textbooks are viewed as presenting information as incontrovertible fact, prohibiting discussion and the sharing of ideas among students. Dependence on textbooks discourages development of critical-thinking skills and hands-on, active involvement of students in their own learning.

Teaching from a perspective that encourages critical thinking should lead students to develop concepts for understanding science and other content areas that they can use throughout their lives, for personal use and in the workplace. Science and math education should make students competent problem solvers, able to think critically and confident in their science and mathematical abilities.

Reducing dependence on textbooks that emphasize rote memorization and facts learned in isolation frees students from memorizing facts and definitions unrelated to any prior knowledge they may have about the subject. Too often, it has been found, science textbooks do not encourage a mindset conducive to scientific inquiry because they do not build on what students already know about a subject (Santa and

Alvermann, 1991). Rather, new material tends to be presented in isolation, without reference to what students may have studied in prior textbook chapters or even in earlier grades (Rutherford and Ahlgren, 1990; Santa and Alvermann, 1991). Too often there is no overarching theme or "major storyline" (National Research Council, 1994, p. 4) that would help children see the interconnectedness and unity of the science curriculum across all the science content domains.

In identifying the content of the new science standards as general categories, no attempt is made to identify specific learning units. Rather, the emphasis is on integrating science with all areas of the curriculum. The committee recommends teaching basic content material that is representative of broad scientific principles and, at the same time, is meaningful to the common, everyday experiences of children. Further, the subject matter should be based on a limited number of concepts that are fundamental to all science learning because of their capacity to explain, probe, and predict other science concepts, principles, and theories and call forth further questions when necessary (National Research Council, 1994).

A major complaint about existing science curricula is that they present science as a completed subject without reference to ongoing explorations in most scientific fields. Textbooks do not present the excitement of scientists exploring and discovering new ideas, proving and disproving proposed theories. Science content is presented as a finished product with little or no reference to the search for evidence to support new information and theories. Students are given little opportunity to learn to think like scientists and ask probing questions about evidence to support new theories, to learn how to make inferences based on what is now known, or to know that it is accepted procedure to accept, modify, or discard conclusions that don't fit their investigations. The standards refer repeatedly to thinking skills, creative solutions, and secondary materials to encourage the development of scientific literacy. Books, reference materials, databases, and other media are cited as making important contributions in this effort.

Implementing the Standards with Trade Books

In contrast to textbooks, trade books explore a single topic in depth and give readers an exhilarating point of view, a personal voice of the author, who wants to communicate and share information with readers. Patricia Lauber in *The News about Dinosaurs* (1989, Bradbury) shares with readers current inquiries and findings from explorations about dinosaurs and scientists' ongoing efforts to learn more about dinosaurs, a subject popular with children. She lets readers see that scientists are always willing to revise their hypotheses as their scientific inquiries yield new information and old theories are disproved.

Don Lessem in *Dinosaur Worlds: New Dinosaurs, New Discoveries* (1996, Boyds Mills Press) provides readers with a similar perspective on scientists—how they pursue new knowledge and how existing hypotheses are revised as new information about dinosaurs is discovered (Figure 2-1). Each of the book's four sections deals with a different prehistoric era. Lessem organizes each section with a historical look back in time, so children have a context for understanding the environment in each of the eras. Current photographs of each geographical area help children understand how scientists pursue fossil clues as they are uncovered. Sidebar charts and illustrations also help make the information more comprehensible. Lessem continues by providing readers with well-organized segments in each section connecting dinosaurs with animals living today in each of the areas described. Finally, he ends each section with a discussion he calls "How Do We Know?" where the work of paleontologists and their colleagues is discussed. The painstaking trial-and-error labors of real scientists are described, making the text more authentic for young readers. Words like "perhaps," "scientists think," and "may have been" show that scientists proceed from an inquiry base, are open-minded, and are willing to revise their hypotheses as new discoveries are made. Sentences such as "Good scientific theories are based on evidence" (Lessem, 1996, p. 45)

FIGURE 2-1 **Nests containing eggs of the Late Cretaceous dinosaur *Oviraptor* has been found throughout the Gobi Desert in Mongolia. When first discovered, these eggs were wrongly thought to be those of *Protoceratops*. Oviraptor was named "egg thief" because scientists thought it was preying on these eggs. New finds of Oviraptor embryos in the eggs and four Oviraptor adults on top of the nest show that this dinosaur was the parent, not a predator, of these eggs.**

Source: Reproduced with permission from Boyds Mills Press.

appear throughout the book, a far cry from presenting scientific data in a sterile manner as if scientists already know all there is about the subject and there are no further discoveries to be made. Lessem's enthusiasm for his subject is clear on every page of *Dinosaur Worlds.*

In *Surtsey, the Newest Place on Earth,* author Kathryn Lasky (1992, Hyperion) and photographer Christopher Knight show the excitement of scientists at work observing, measuring, calculating so that children can see scientists in the field pursuing those activities they are being encouraged to do in the classroom as valid science activities. Such books also show how various science domains are connected to each other, how following the process of scientific inquiry is a creative process representing unity and interconnectedness of thought.

Brightly colored picture books by Gail Gibbons, for example, allow young students in grades K–4 to observe and classify objects they might not otherwise be able to see in the classroom. In *Spiders* by Gail Gibbons (1993, Morrow) large, accurate illustrations are labeled showing body parts, and information about different types of spiders is related in language that is accessible to beginning readers. The author is clearly not afraid of spiders and finds them useful, interesting creatures.

An understanding of how science can contribute to reconciling controversial issues is presented in *Living in a Risky World* by Laurence Pringle (1989, Morrow). Pringle emphasizes the role of scientific inquiry and technological advances leading to improvements in the environment and the workplace. He describes how, building on existing information, scientists are often able to uncover hazards to society and then work to eradicate them. His book shows the importance of scientific inquiry in our everyday lives and the social and ethical impact of scientific endeavors in real-life situations.

MATHEMATICS—TEACHING STANDARDS AND CURRENT THEORY

Traditionally, mathematics teaching has emphasized computational skills based on a textbook-driven curriculum. Students have been routinely drilled in memorizing basic rules and procedures for computing correct answers. As with criticisms of the traditional science curriculum, educators believe that students do not learn to reason and to see math as a problem-solving activity that has relevance for all content areas of the curriculum. Current textbooks and teaching methods are criticized for teaching math as a series of memorization activities within a matrix of rote procedures. Contrary to modern educational theory, which views children as active constructors of knowledge (Piaget, 1970; Vygotsky, 1962) who take responsibility for their own learning, math is currently taught as a series of lock-step procedures in which reasoning, estimating, and problem solving play no part. Students, in fact, often express the skeptical view that learning math has little useful relevance to real-life situations they might encounter.

Before deciding what content should be taught or how it should be taught, the commission on Teaching Standards for Mathematics (NCTM, 1990) explored the concept of mathematical literacy, just as the American Academy for the Advancement of Science started by defining scientific literacy. The importance of mathematical literacy is set within the context of the twenty first–century information-age, computer-driven workplace that is rapidly replacing the industrial age, factory workplace where workers did not need to think and solve problems to get their jobs done. The information age, with its reliance on technological methods and materials, requires workers who understand sophisticated problem-solving strategies based on logic, reason, and critical thinking. Also, workers now have to be prepared for lifelong learning, as new technologies are introduced and existing jobs become obsolete. They have to be competent at mathematical reasoning, problem solving, and communicating mathematical ideas and functions as well as being technologically competent.

The committee responsible for preparing the new math standards defined mathematical literacy *for all students* as learning to value math, to use mathematical reasoning to solve problems, to be confident in the ability to perform mathematical operations, and to be able to communicate mathematical ideas. Specifically, mathematical literacy is defined as denoting "an individual's abilities to explore, to conjecture, and to reason logically, as well as to use a variety of mathematical methods effectively to solve problems. By becoming literate, their mathematical power should develop" (NCTM, 1989, p. 6). Further, the mathematically literate person will perceive math as a system for communicating coherently and confidently.

A series of picture books by Stuart Murphy ("MathStart," 1996, HarperCollins), based on the new math standards written by the National Council of Teachers of Mathematics (1989), presents a series of real-life situations familiar to young children. In each of the books, illustrated in bright primary colors, children read about problems they frequently confront. Several possible solutions are discussed and discarded until it is clear why only one solution is correct. Rather than presenting each problem as a narrowly focused computation problem, the stories illustrate math concepts in text and pictures. The visual aspect of each story clearly demonstrates and reinforces the math concept being presented.

Children in the primary grades can see why each situation is a problem and can visually follow along until the solution is found. For instance, in the first book for the youngest students, *A Pair of Socks* (Murphy, 1996), the concept of matching socks to make a pair starts with one lone sock lamenting its plight as readers accompany it on its search, rejecting near look-alikes until its mate is found. Readers are asked whether they agree or disagree that each sock is the missing part of the pair. Activities are suggested at the end of the book for reinforcing the concept, such as children drawing pairs of matching items, finding pairs of things in the classroom, and bringing pairs of items from home. The concept of pairs is then extended to several content areas, such as finding pairs in nature and identifying rhythms that create a repeated pattern in music.

Approaching math this way demystifies it and shows that "doing" math is really an everyday activity that is part of everyone's life, an activity that we do all day long. A brother and sister figuring out how to divide a pizza or cookies in half so they can share equally is a situation familiar to children everywhere. Murphy uses it as the humorous subject of *Give Me Half!* (1996) as he deals with an important mathematical concept.

Another title in the "MathStart" series, *Get Up and Go* (Murphy, 1996), presents the concept of time lines in a graphic, concrete way by depicting the minutes a child needs to get ready for school in the morning. The minutes she spends snuggling her teddy bear are shown in purple and the minutes washing are shown in red segments. The two activities are then shown together in their respective colors in one line, and readers are asked to count how many minutes have passed. The cumulative story allows readers to see the brightly segmented time line getting longer as the child gets ready for school. Finally, the completed time line is shown on a double-page spread with the corresponding number of minutes printed above the time line. Children can count the distinctly colored minute segments on the time line or add the numbers printed above the line to see how long it took to get ready for school. (See Figure 2-2.)

Many excellent trade books encourage the development of math problem-solving skills as recommended in *Curriculum and Evaluation Standards for School Mathematics* (NCTM, 1989). One that children particularly enjoy, which they see as a game, is *Math Curse* by Jon Scieszka and Lane Smith (1995, Viking), a popular author-illustrator team. This slim, oversized volume is intended for an older reading audience than is the "MathStart" series. It begins by presenting math problems, probability problems, and math symbols on the book jacket and continues through the dedication and right on into the text as readers follow a young girl through a school day seeing how even choosing which dress to wear can be stated as an inquiry problem in mathematical language. Solutions are presented on the back cover, but make sure a new version of the book is used—a fifth-grade honors class worked out all the problems and was able to prove another solution to one of them (M. Kayden, personal communication, Dec. 5, 1995)!

The standards emphasize that, to develop mathematical literacy, students need to develop a historical appreciation of math's value in world events. They also need to have an understanding of math's value in the information age and the relationship of mathematics to other content areas such as science, history, the arts, music, and the social sciences. Students learn best when the learning is relevant to their lives, whether in math or any other content area. When students have a purpose for learning, their learning becomes meaningful, useful, and thorough.

By stipulating that students have frequent and numerous opportunities to use math in practical, useful settings, the standards (NCTM, 1989) anticipate that students will develop confidence in their ability to successfully perform

She's already late—so I'd better try
to keep careful track of the time going by.

I can show her 5-minute snuggle with Teddy like this.

3 minutes to wash looks like this.

Now I'll put my lines together.

How many minutes have gone by so far?

FIGURE 2-2 Illustration from *Get Up and Go*

Source: Text copyright © 1996 by Stuart J. Murphy. Illustrations copyright © 1996 by Diana Greenseid. MathStart is a trademark of HarperCollins Publishers.

mathematical calculations and apply mathematical thinking in new situations. Students need to see math as a problem-solving discipline with relevance for all human endeavors. Mathematical problem solving, like science problem solving, needs to be taught as a hands-on experience that may extend over a period of time and involve using a variety of sources in the solution rather than a traditional set of simple calculations assigned to be completed in a single class session. The standards (NCTM, 1989) discuss the necessity of encouraging students to consult a variety of book and nonbook media sources in their problem-solving efforts, along with the use of calculators and other electronic media when appropriate.

As in other content disciplines, the recent standards for math call for giving students opportunities to be active participants in their own learning through employing strategies that have them interact with their physical world, familiar materials, and their classmates (NCTM, 1989). In such an atmosphere it is expected that students will explore, test, and discuss concepts and relationships about math with each other as they come to understand the abstract ideas embedded in manipulating materials.

It is further recommended that, as appropriate, students be given opportunities to work cooperatively either in small groups or as a whole class. Such an approach is consistent with recommendations of other educators for teaching math (Davidson, 1990; Wood, 1992) and other content subjects as well.

All kinds of materials should be available in the classroom for math learning, from simple geometric figures and shapes to household objects to sophisticated scientific calculators and computers. The standards (NCTM, 1989) repeatedly stress that children need hands-on experiences with materials that relate to real problems they encounter in their lives. In this way they will come to understand mathematics' role in their lives and become actively involved in learning math.

As students progress in their problem-solving abilities and have frequent opportunities to read, write, and discuss mathematical ideas, they should become familiar with the specialized vocabulary and symbols of mathematics. Through this process, students would be expected to achieve fluency in communicating ideas mathematically (NCTM, 1989), a necessity in the modern workplace and in communicating via technological media. Children should be encouraged to communicate their thoughts about math problems and situations, record and summarize data, hypothesize, and write their observations and conclusions. It is recommended that they write in math journals just as they do in other content area journals. Writing to clarify their thoughts promotes learning the language of math and encourages the development of problem-solving and reasoning skills. In math, as in other subjects, writing should be viewed as a process that gives students the opportunity to brainstorm, clarify, and revise their writing (Calkins, 1986; Graves, 1983; Hansen, 1987). In mathematics, writing has the added benefit of allowing students to explain a math problem they are working on and encourages positive attitudes about math (NCTM, 1989).

A final aspect of mathematical literacy is important for its significance across the curriculum; this final goal of mathematical literacy has to do with learning to reason mathematically. There is evidence that if students can be taught to think critically about math problems they are trying to solve, their ability to use reasoning skills to solve problems will have a profound effect on other areas of their learning as well. Posing hypotheses, gathering evidence, and constructing a coherent argument are all examples of thinking like a mathematician—evidence of mathematical literacy.

SOCIAL STUDIES—THEORY AND CURRICULUM STANDARDS

A task force of the National Council for the Social Studies has recently completed and published a set of curriculum standards to be used as a guideline for teaching social studies. The document, *Expectations of Excellence: Curriculum Standards for the Social Studies* (1994, NCSS), includes a scope and sequence curriculum plan from kindergarten through grade 12 and recommendations for achieving those expectations.

The social studies standards are organized around students acquiring a cluster of related cognitive skills and an associated set of values that foster democratic behaviors and responsible citizenship. Because "social studies" encompasses a multitude of diverse disciplines, the following subjects are addressed in the standards: anthropology, archaeology, civics, economics, geography, government, history, law, philosophy, psychology, religion, and sociology. In preparing the standards there was also general agreement about which strategic skills needed by students are critical to learning in this content area. They are identified as: reading maps; interpreting charts, tables, and graphs; following a time line and sequence of events; recognizing propaganda; understanding cause and effect; conducting simple survey research and statistical analyses; and being able to distinguish fact from opinion. These are all skills that a good social studies program helps students learn. Curriculum standards formulated by the National Council for the Social Studies (1994) focus on preparing students to take their place as members of a democratic society, intent on supporting ideals expressed in the preamble to the U.S. Constitution.

The social studies standards seek to achieve their goals through those methodologies acknowledged as being most effective in recent research studies. The goals are traditional ones that inculcate democratic beliefs and values in students as well as help prepare them to live and work in the global village of the twenty-first century. The curriculum standards offer students varied opportunities to engage in social inquiry and make connections between what they know, new skills they are learning, and a sense of values rooted in democratic traditions (NCSS, 1994). Ten thematic strands are identified as appropriate study areas at all grade levels; for each of these strands the necessity of providing students with high-quality resources and materials including the finest children's trade books is repeatedly emphasized. Active learning—having students involved in problem-solving and decision-making processes while learning to recognize historical themes and making connections across other disciplines they study—is seen as vital to a successful social studies curriculum. As in other subject areas, it is emphasized that students need to be technologically prepared to locate, analyze, interpret, and evaluate information from a variety of sources.

Ten concepts related to social studies themes that are appropriate at all grade levels are identified as curriculum model units along with standards that describe expected learning outcomes. Within each of the ten themes and at all grade levels, students are expected to learn a variety of strategies for acquiring, organizing, and using information, along with the ability to work cooperatively within a group. Basic values such as respect for individual rights, freedoms, and citizens' and government's responsibilities are included within the standard for the scope of each theme.

The first thematic strand explores aspects of similarity and diversity among cultures and nations through reading children's books that exemplify this theme or through a similar literature-related activity. The theme of the second standard deals with time, continuity, and change. The standards (NCSS, 1993) suggest that one way to study this theme is through reading stories about the past or diaries, letters, and documents detailing first-hand accounts of past events. As in the science and math content area standards, it is recommended that writing process activities such as personal response journals coordinate with reading trade books and primary source materials. These activities allow students to interpret, evaluate, and analyze what they are reading, all of which is basic to teaching students to be critical readers and thinkers. Space and place, the third theme, is intended to foster the acquisition of a sense of geography, the importance of caring for the environment, the ability to use tools and resources such as maps and atlases, and the manipulation of technology such as computer databases.

Reading a variety of print materials such as trade books, atlases, journals, specialized reference books, newspapers, and periodicals is an integral part of each of the ten thematic strands of the curriculum standards in social studies (1994). Strands of the recommended curriculum include units on individual development and identity; production, distribution, and consumption; power, authority, and governance; citizenship; and global connections. These units employ the tenet of reading across the curriculum; writing is recognized as an adjunct to the reading program and students are expected to be given the opportunity to write in a variety of formats. Many social studies themes recommend that, in order to share ideas and employ the concept of collaborative learning, students have opportunities to work together in small groups solving problems relating to the curriculum and describing the ideas, issues, and theories they encounter.

The prototype unit on science, technology, and society recommends that students have multiple opportunities at all grade levels to understand the relationship between science and technology and the social studies. In the early grades, manipulating various technologies such as computer databases for accessing and retrieving information is emphasized; at the upper grades a study of the impact of technology on society and the individual is recommended.

CONTENT AREA LEARNING AND CRITICAL THINKING

Each of the content areas previously discussed emphasizes the importance of thinking skills related to reading and writing strategies across the curriculum. A classic definition of critical thinking is provided by Ennis (1985) as "reasonable, reflective thinking that is focused on deciding what to believe" (p. 54). This is generally interpreted as including thinking processes that can be labeled "reasonable" when the discerning reader/thinker carefully analyzes text looking for valid evidence to support the author's thesis and arguments and is able to reach logical, relevant conclusions. Critical reading and thinking means the reader thinks carefully about the text being read, isn't in a hurry to reach conclusions, and considers opposing points of views. Critical thinkers should be able to practice the traditional "willing suspension of disbelief" until they have finished reading and considering all the information in the text. Students become critical readers when they read with open minds able to think about conflicting viewpoints, seek evidence to support the author's claims, and reach objective conclusions.

It is widely held that students at all grade levels can benefit from instruction and practice in using the aptitudes labeled "critical-thinking skills." These techniques are especially helpful when students need to read content area expository text. If reading is viewed as a thinking activity

(Rumelhart, 1984), then fluent readers who read with great comprehension, as well as students who struggle with their reading assignments, can understand the components of a critical thinking strategy and learn to apply specific skills associated with this technique.

Many educators and researchers have identified components of critical thinking that all students, with time and practice, can recognize and apply as they read. The principles of critical thinking as identified by Ennis (1987), Gunning (1992), and others include being open-minded so that sources of information can be judged for slanted, biased writing and the use of propaganda techniques; affirming that credible sources have been cited and that the facts as presented are verifiable; drawing logical conclusions based on the material presented and fully supported within the text. Further characteristics of critical thinkers include the ability to distinguish between fact and opinion and recognize code words that express opinions, judgments, and attempts to influence; to identify the thesis or question posed in the text; and, finally, to change one's point of view when evidence in the text is compelling enough to warrant a change.

Critical reading is reading with a spirit of inquiry. In each of the recently published content area teaching standards the authors write about teaching from an inquiry-based learning perspective. Clearly, critical thinking and inquiry-based learning are seen as driving any new curriculum standards for teaching and learning. As the authors of the proposed science standards state (National Research Council, 1994), the curriculum needs revision to teach what is basic to educating a scientifically literate populace, not to encourage more memorization of isolated facts. And the components of critical thinking appear within the definition of scientific literacy.

SUMMARY

Much of the criticism of current teaching practices in the content areas centers around traditional methods that emphasize memorization, drill, and rote learning. These practices are reinforced by an overreliance on textbooks and a lack of hands-on activities. In contrast, the recently adopted standards in each of the content areas emphasize an integrated, hands-on approach to learning the processes and content of science, mathematics, and social studies. All of the content area standards propose that there be less emphasis on drill and skill exercises and more emphasis on learning concepts and the acquisition of critical-thinking skills. As reliance on textbooks diminishes, there is a call for an increase in the use of meaningful, hands-on learning activities and children's trade books that relate learning experiences to real-life situations.

▶ 3

Developing
an Information
Curriculum

During the past ten years, technological resources for storing and retrieving information have been developed that surpass anything formerly available. The new technologies have brought with them new methodologies for information searching that require alternative searching strategies. Activities and services in support of an information curriculum integrate traditional resources and the new technologies to empower students to take responsibility for their own learning, for acquiring a critical-thinking stance, and for applying the processes of scientific inquiry to their own learning in all content areas.

Just as students need access to information, they also need real reasons for wanting to acquire information: they need to develop an attitude for inquiry learning. They enjoy accessing data through computer databases, CD-ROM disks, searching the internet, and other high-tech hardware, but, most importantly, they must first know why they are seeking the information and why it is important to them to learn. Students must have a clear idea of what information they are looking for.

ACQUIRING AN ATTITUDE FOR INQUIRY

Inquiry-based learning in an information-seeking environment requires that children be active constructors of their own knowledge based on their interactions with various media, the physical and symbolic worlds, teachers, and each other. Inquiry learning is a problem-solving process that requires formulating a problem, usually in the form of a question or hypothesis to be answered; making observations; and gathering information about the problem. The final step in the process is developing a reasonable response to the original problem. It might be a logical solution or "answer" to the original problem, a modification of the stated hypothesis, or the conclusion that further study in another direction is required. The answer to one problem may well become the statement of a new problem to study.

Organizing the classroom as a place to learn problem-solving or inquiry techniques is identified by Jerome Harste (Monson and Monson, 1994) as a critical element in preparing students to function effectively in the twenty-first century. Inquiry learning should be the context for learning across the curriculum, encompassing problem-solving strategies that are useful in all disciplines and which prepare students to solve the range of problems they will face in their lifetimes. According to Harste:

> An inquiry curriculum assumes that kids are researchers, that they should be allowed to inquire, and they should be encouraged to go off in directions that may not be predetermined. Real inquiry has to have an open-

ness about it so that people can go in directions and reach conclusions that are unforeseen. (Monson and Monson, 1994, p. 519)

Teachers should point out the possibility that different conclusions can be reached, according to Harste, so that children understand and accept that a wide range of solutions to the original problem is possible. Inquiry learning is facilitated by involving students in hands-on exploration; visiting sites such as museums, libraries, and restorations; handling original documents; manipulating media; and speaking with other people involved in working on the problem. When curriculum is developed through student-generated questions and inquiries, with the teacher guiding students through the content areas, children learn that the content areas are not immutable. They learn that content is not a static body of knowledge to be memorized but is instead something to be explored and that they have a valid voice in that exploration (Monson and Monson, 1994).

Because inquiry learning is an active process in which children need to manipulate media, objects, and symbols in their problem-solving efforts, they need to be able to think critically about the information they gather. They need to continually ask themselves questions about the relevance of material they have collected, what should be retained, and what should be discarded. With a series of questions in mind that relate to the larger problem being studied, children focus on what is relevant and think critically about whether or not the information being retrieved is helpful to their investigation of the main problem being studied.

Inquiry-Based Learning in Science

As the teacher you need to model this approach to learning. An example of teachers modeling inquiry-based learning behaviors for their students appears in Molly Cone's book *Come Back Salmon* (1992, Sierra Club Books). Several teachers take their classes into the field to show them first-hand a stream's devastation brought about by pollution and neglect. The problem posed by Mr. King, one of the fifth-grade teachers, was whether or not Pigeon Creek in Washington state could be cleaned up and brought back to life. Even the school principal became involved in the inquiry by contacting the Adopt-A-Stream Foundation to provide support and guidance for the project, which ultimately involved all the students at Jackson Elementary School.

Cone's book relates how the students' initial skepticism about whether they could make a difference and help restore the stream to a healthy environment was overcome by the teacher's modeling of the inquiry process. Mr. King took his class to the polluted stream to observe the problem first-hand. This on-site visit generated many questions from the children and gave them an opportunity to search for and gather information at the primary source. Children were able to see how much work was necessary to restore the stream to its pristine condition, and they could not yet envision restoring the stream as a habitat for spawning salmon. As the inquiry proceeded into the problem of whether or not the stream could be cleaned up and further pollution halted, additional problems were generated for the students.

As a first step the children went back to the stream and tried to remove debris that had collected there. When this turned out to be a daunting task, the children asked about alternative solutions. With their teachers' encouragement they planned alternative strategies that included lobbying their city council to change its plans for building a storage facility at the creek's mouth. As they continued the search for ways to solve their problem and learn about the delicate balance of conditions needed to sustain life in a freshwater environment, Mr. King encouraged his students to keep searching for solutions by reminding them, "You can make a difference" (Cone, 1992, p. 17). Children came to accept the problem of saving the stream as a real-life situation and to believe that their problem-solving strategies could really make a difference. The book cites many instances of the children thinking critically about how they were proceeding and about whether measures they wanted to adopt to save the creek were consistent with their goals and would produce positive results. They retained what was relevant to solving their problem, such as frequent patrols of the creek bank to keep it free from discarded debris, and abandoned efforts that were futile.

As the students worked on their problem, they were learning the vocabulary of ecological science and the salmon life cycle and spawning habits. The book details how each grade learned these things by following an appropriate curriculum that allowed them to value their own participation in the project. They used all possible learning modes: They did research and read from many sources and media forms; they handled objects and manipulated scientific equipment and measuring tools; they presented their message in words, signs, and symbols. At each step along the way their classroom teachers encouraged students to believe that they could indeed effect a solution and helped them consider the solutions to alternative problems that arose as they worked. When students observed there was a problem in the tank where the salmon were kept, they were able to apply their problem-solving strategies and newly acquired knowledge about the importance of oxygen and clean water to rescue the salmon. This was one of many instances when they were able to apply what they were learning in several content areas to a real-life, practical situation. It was immediately clear to the children that what they were inquiring and researching about had practical applications beyond getting the correct answer on a test.

Content area classes such as science, math, art, and social studies focused on aspects of ecology or the life cycle of salmon that were relevant to the restoration of Pigeon Creek. The youngest classes created posters reminding people not to pollute the stream, and older children handed out leaflets in the community. They wrote their own books telling what they had learned about the habits of salmon based on research they conducted. All of these efforts helped students to learn not only the "facts" about salmon and ecology but, more importantly, about how seemingly esoteric academic subjects have real-life significance for individuals and whole communities. No longer was the salmon's life cycle merely one more chapter in their science textbooks; now it was something they were learning about from a hands-on perspective. They were actively involved in finding a solution to a problem that affected the entire community, and they knew they were the most significant part of the solution. This is real learning, learning students can take into adulthood and use all their lives in many other situations. It is not based on finding a predetermined "correct answer"; it is a curriculum that is process-oriented, that puts students in charge of their own learning and enables them to develop insights and strategies for solving problems that will be useful throughout their lifetimes.

Inquiry-Based Learning in the Social Studies

The same sort of inquiry approach to learning can be used in the social studies content area. Let us choose a subject we would like our students to think about and to learn more about. First, take a look around your classroom. Your students' faces most likely reflect the diversity of the current U.S. population. Many of them may be recent arrivals in the United States, and English may not be the language spoken at home. Therefore, let us consider immigration as a social studies topic to explore using an inquiry approach to learning. In this section we shall see how an inquiry approach can be used to generate questions for students to investigate.

To help children acquire an attitude for inquiry, you can initiate a class discussion about what is happening in the United States today, asking children if they have heard about the plight of "boat people" from various countries, the evacuation of children from the war-ravaged Balkan countries, and whether they have heard their grandparents or other relatives speak about coming to the United States. Some children may be aware of the national debate about limiting the rights to work, to education, and to health care for new immigrants; others may have heard proposals to make English our official language; and they may have questions about what this all means.

There is a difference between assigning topics for report writing and having children investigate something perceived of as a genuine problem. In a traditional teacher-centered classroom, children would be assigned to gather information and write reports telling everything they have found about immigration. Learning about immigration as an inquiry-based research topic means that children research and report back to the class about specific problems and questions of interest to them, such as what U.S. policy has been concerning immigration, what immigration laws have been passed, how many immigrants have come from which different countries in which decades. When a subject is posed as a problem, as a series of student-generated questions for them to inquire about, children take control of their own learning and think critically about what information they need to gather, what questions to ask, and where and how to gather the information (Monson and Monson, 1994). As they proceed, students have to decide what information is relevant to solving the problem and what is not and to continue formulating pertinent questions.

In the primary grades the questions might arise from something you are reading aloud to the class. As you read, children may come directly to you with their questions, or they may ask the class at circle or sharing time. Several trade books are first-rate "read-alouds" that can introduce the subject of immigration and what it feels like to come to a new country. *Immigrant Kids* (1980, Dutton), Russell Freedman's photographic essay of children who came to this country at the turn of the century, shows what life was like in school, at home, and at play for young immigrants as they sought to learn the customs of their new country. Its authentic archival photographs and Freedman's lively writing will inspire your students to ask many questions and make numerous comparisons with their own lives today. This should set them on a course of discovery leading to inquiring from primary sources such as their parents, grandparents, and people in the neighborhood. Doubtless there will be children in the class who have their own memories of coming to this country and who will be able to provide classmates with a personal perspective on what the immigrant experience is like today.

Another book that will stimulate children's curiosity and lead them to want to know more is Leonard Everett Fisher's *Ellis Island* (1986, Holiday House). The journey of fifteen million immigrants who came to this country between 1892 and 1954 is told with lavish illustrations, archival photographs, and excerpts from letters and diaries. Reading like an exciting narrative, the story draws readers in and stirs their imaginations with the opening words: "America fever!" (Fisher, 1986, p. 7). The author then explains some of the reasons these early immigrants came to the United States. The text should stimulate your students to ask questions about current patterns of immigration and why people seek to enter the United States today.

The line between narrative and expository text for children becomes more blurred each year. Books that would formerly have been published as traditional narrative texts often have their basis in one or more incidents that actually took place or are about real characters but are written with a recognizable story format. Three books in this category tell about incidents in the lives of their authors' relatives and are effective in helping young students develop positive attitudes toward inquiry learning. *Molly's Pilgrim* by Barbara Cohen (1983, Lothrop, Lee & Shepard) tells the story of a young Russian immigrant and her embarrassment at being different from her classmates. Set early in the century when being different and speaking with an accent were less acceptable and the emphasis was on adopting American customs and dress as quickly as possible, the story tells of Molly's discomfort when the children in her class tease her about her foreign ways. When Molly's mother helps her make a doll for the class Thanksgiving celebration, she finally wins acceptance and is more secure of her own place in school and the community. She learns that Pilgrims come from many places and different eras, each one making a unique contribution to American culture, each one thankful to be here.

American Too by Elisa Bartone (1996, Lothrop, Lee & Shepard), with illustrations by Ted Lewin, is set in the same era as *Molly's Pilgrim* and tells a similar story of an immigrant child who finds her own way of becoming an American citizen. Rosina has recently arrived from Italy, and her family has settled in New York City's "little Italy" section. In this sensitive story based on a real incident in the author's family, Rosina is teased by her American-born classmates and made to feel embarrassed because of her foreign-sounding speech and dress and the unfamiliar foods she brings to school for lunch. The illustrations and text help readers feel Rosina's anguish while she tries to adapt to American culture. Finally, as queen of the San Gennaro festival where she dresses as the Statue of Liberty, Rosina realizes she can keep the best of both cultures. The narrative quietly explores the theme of who is an American and what makes an American, until Rosina laughs with the realization that "Anything is possible in America."

Another picture book that sensitively relates the immigrant experience is the 1994 Caldecott Medal book *Grandfather's Journey* by Allen Say (1993, Houghton Mifflin). Here Say, the author and illustrator, has captured the universal emotions of the immigrant experience. He describes his grandfather's settling in California, bringing his Japanese bride here, and making a life for himself while being ever homesick for his native land. He and his family travel back to Japan, where the author was born at the start of World War II. Say lives and works in the United States now but travels to Japan frequently because, as he writes, "I can not still the longing in my heart" for one country as soon as he settles into his other homeland. Children who have memories of life in another place or who have heard parents and grandparents talk about life in another country will recognize these sentiments and relate to the story on an intimate basis. Each of these books, suitable for reading aloud all through the elementary grades for the content they relate, will provoke varied responses from students while raising many questions for further study about the immigrant experience and how Americans have responded to newly arrived immigrants.

GENERATING QUESTIONS TO EXPLORE

As students respond to evocative stories, they will discover how broad a topic is and how it cuts across all traditional academic disciplines. As a facilitator you may need to help your students explore different aspects relating to immigration so that the extent of the inquiry to be investigated becomes clear. In this way small groups can work together on various aspects of the topic and report back to the class with the results of their inquiries. You may also encourage students to consider all the appropriate content areas if they have missed a potential area of exploration. For instance, after reading *Grandfather's Journey,* students may wonder about the difficulties of adjusting to life in a new country, eating new foods, and celebrating new holidays. If the question is not raised, you would raise the issue of new immigrants returning to their countries of origin, asking a group of students to inquire if this was a common occurrence and what kind of numbers support whatever conclusion the inquiry reveals. Exploring the concept of immigration from one homeland to another should provide students with more than the facts about immigration; it should give them the tools to pursue solutions using all the possible disciplines to reach a series of understandings about the subject.

In discussing student responses to the stories, you need to ask questions that are genuine, questions that require students to respond with information that is not explicitly stated. Asking why the author's grandfather chose to return to Japan or why Molly felt excluded from the class's Thanksgiving celebration requires students to think in broader terms than merely recalling the story's events. These are real questions that invite all students in the class to respond, that respect the opinions of all students, and that elicit responses that are nonjudgmental.

In a brainstorming session after reading *Immigrant Kids* or *Ellis Island,* questions that you might ask to initiate an inquiry-based learning experience are: How are these children coping with learning a new language, new customs, new holidays? What should schools, communities, social agencies do to help these children and their families adjust to life in a new society? Should new immigrants surrender their old ways, learn to speak English only? Should we strive to be a melting pot or, in the words of a former mayor of New York City, a "gorgeous mosaic"? Should the United States continue to broaden its immigration policies and admit people of diverse colors and races who are different from the original European colonists? And, finally, how has the United States historically welcomed great masses of immigrants? Questions such as these help children to understand that there are many aspects to the topic and to focus on a particular aspect of immigration that they want to investigate. Children realize that this is not simply a topic in their textbook that you have to assign; rather, this is a real-life topic of critical importance for the community and the nation. This look around the classroom provides clear evidence that one open-ended question can generate an entire curriculum for inquiry-based learning that allows children to be active constructors of their own knowledge. The questions you pose and those the children come forward with are real questions that relate to trying to solve a problem and that respect children's efforts as problem solvers rather than as recallers of details from stories.

Helping children ask significant questions requires that you help them acquire good listening skills. They need to focus their attention on what you are reading to them and on class discussions that follow. Like the reading process, it is as important that the listening process lead to comprehension and understanding. Jean Craighead George's book *The*

First Thanksgiving (1993, Philomel) presents many ideas about the earliest European immigrants to the "New World" and the Native Americans already there that may be startling to elementary school children. Before reading the book to your class, it would be helpful to discuss with the children why it is important for them to listen attentively. Tell them you want them to hear more than the words you will read—you want them to listen for the ideas in the story. Explain to them that this story contains new information about why the Pilgrims left England and sought refuge in the New World; about the treatment of the local New England tribes; and about how the new immigrants, without the Native Americans' help, would have perished that first winter in Plymouth. Despite its picture book format, this informational book is packed with accurate historical data that might otherwise be missed if children were not guided about how to listen and what to listen for.

Children used to cheery (sanitized) stories about the early settlers will need you to provide them with a framework for listening. Before reading *Sarah Morton's Day* by Kate Waters (1989, Scholastic), a pictorial account of a young girl's day of work and play in Plymouth Colony, explain to the class your purpose for reading this book. Telling the children that you want them to hear what Sarah's jobs were and what games she played sets a specific purpose for listening and focuses children's attention on what they should especially listen for.

To reinforce good listening habits, after reading to your class, encourage the children to share their ideas about what you have read by asking open-ended questions such as how would they feel if they had to do Sarah's chores and memorize sections of scripture, or how would they feel living in a new place and missing the comforts they had before coming to the New World. Lucille Recht Penner's *Eating the Plates: A Pilgrim Book of Food and Manners* (1991, Macmillan) spans both social studies and science as it presents recipes, eating customs, and the Pilgrim's beliefs about foods. As you prepare your class to listen to the book, direct their attention to the ingredients used in preparing food and to the descriptions of the Pilgrims' table manners, such as discouraging diners from removing fleas and lice from their clothes while at the table. Afterward, during class sharing of responses to the book, probe their responses by encouraging them to talk about the book with prompts such as, "Tell us more" and "Why do you think that?" As children learn to anticipate such questions, they will learn to focus their attention and listen carefully while you read.

Initiating an inquiry-based search for information should be a two-way avenue of communication between you and your students. While there is a prescribed curriculum you are responsible for teaching, children also have valid questions to ask that may spark an exciting inquiry search. Children's questions often come from the books they read; to encourage them to read widely on a subject and consult a variety of sources as they seek answers to their questions is to encourage the most meaningful kind of learning.

Encouraging children to ask questions tells them that, like adult researchers and scientists, they too are learners and inquirers. In order to support children asking questions, you can share with them several books in which the authors show that scientists and researchers needed to ask many questions because the answers weren't known. *The News about Dinosaurs* by Patricia Lauber reveals that scientists must keep an open and inquiring mind, willing to accommodate new information when it becomes available. Lauber contrasts old hypotheses about dinosaurs with adjustments scientists make in their thinking as a result of new information gleaned through first-hand exploration in the field. She does this by using several critical phrases you want to be sure your students notice as models for their own thinking and writing: "Scientists used to think...", "For many years, people thought..." (Lauber, 1989, p. 12). She uses words like *wondered, perhaps, must have, feel sure,* and *have found* (Lauber, 1989); all of these words, in context, show children that scientists are learning all the time and modifying their theories to accommodate new discoveries. In large capital letters and contrasting color print, Lauber trumpets "THE NEWS IS: ..." to let children know that new information has been discovered, leading scientists to modify or discard old beliefs about dinosaurs. She ends the book with the notice that there is still more left to discover and learn about dinosaurs—that science is not a closed subject. All of Lauber's techniques can be used in the classroom for science and other content area studies. Your class can write a book with small groups each contributing some information they have researched and written in this style: What we thought we knew before and what we know now. Use of such a technique clarifies new learning for children and shows them that all learning involves modifying prior beliefs (schema) as new information is learned.

Another book that introduces readers to the idea that doing research often leads to modification of prior knowledge and beliefs is James Cross Giblin's *The Riddle of the Rosetta Stone: Key to Ancient Egypt* (1990, Crowell). In describing how the ancient hieroglyphs were painstakingly decoded, Giblin explains how a succession of social scientists and scholars worked patiently, frequently eliminating what they thought they had deciphered and starting again over the course of two hundred years. This reads like an intriguing mystery story while it shows children the course of meticulous scientific investigation. This book can also be used as a model for children to pursue their own content area inquiries and for learning what questions to ask.

INFORMATION-GATHERING STRATEGIES

Once a topic to be explored has been agreed upon and groups of children have chosen subtopics to inquire about and research, the process of researching a topic and gathering information should be reviewed with your students. As a former school library media specialist, my first recommendation would be to inform your school's media specialist that your class is about to start a research project. The media specialist will help you plan an inquiry search, check to see what sources of information are available in different media, suggest which media your students should use for their searches, and recommend strategies for successfully accessing the media center's resources. Usually one or more sessions will be scheduled for your class to review the media center's resources and explain to students how to initiate a successful media search for information.

There are four elements involved in conducting a successful inquiry research project: (1) searching for, selecting, accessing, and retrieving information; (2) analyzing and evaluating information; (3) synthesizing information; and (4) communicating information. It is a complex process that, when broken down into its component parts, can be comfortably negotiated by even the youngest elementary school students. In this section we shall discuss information-gathering strategies related to searching for and selecting information and techniques for accessing and retrieving the data selected.

Searching for and Selecting Information

Children need instruction to learn how to plan and initiate a research inquiry project focusing on problem-solving strategies. It should start with a collaborative brainstorming session that gives every child in the class an opportunity to contribute suggestions. One activity that works well at this point is to prepare a *K-W-L* chart (Ogle, 1986) that will remain visible in the classroom for the duration of the inquiry project (see Figure 3-1). With this brainstorming strategy you visually represent *K*—What We Know; *W*—What We Want to Know (before they start their inquiry projects); and *L*—What We Have Learned, which allows children to evaluate their own learning at the conclusion of their work. This strategy helps children set a clear purpose for their research.

Brainstorming and using the *K-W-L* strategy allow for the recall of any prior knowledge children may have about the various topics that have been suggested. Children who have a keen interest in a particular topic will be able to support each other's interests and will most likely work well together to produce a final project that reflects their enthusiasm. Conducting several collaborative brainstorming sessions will also allow you to assess how well acquainted the children are with the proposed inquiry topic and which questions the children want to find out more about. At this point you will want to check with the school library media specialist to see which topics are well represented in the library's book and media collections so your students will not be frustrated in their search for information.

Browsing Strategies

Once a list of several topics has been generated for the class to consider and you have created a wall or blackboard chart of these proposals, children should visit the media center to verify that their proposals are valid topics for inquiry. They can do this by browsing through the reference and circulating collections and other media to see what materials are

FIGURE 3-1 **K-W-L Strategy Chart about Immigration**

_K_—What We Know	_W_—What We Want to Know	_L_—What We Have Learned
Many new immigrants do not speak English when they first come to the U.S.	Why do people leave their country to come to the U.S.; are there different reasons?	

Many new immigrants do not speak English when they first come to the U.S.

It is scary to leave your country and family to come to a new country.

New immigrants are often comfortable living together in the same neighborhood.

Some immigrants face discrimination because they don't speak English or they look different.

All of us came from somewhere else at one time.

Some people don't want any new immigrants to come here.

Many Americans who came here as immigrants became famous.

Over the years there have been changes in the areas of the world where new immigrants come from.

Immigrants need permission to work but children can go to school.

Why do people leave their country to come to the U.S.; are there different reasons?

Is it hard to get a job, go to school and make friends when someone doesn't speak English?

Do immigrants have to wait a long time before they are allowed to come to the U.S.?

Do most immigrants keep their old customs and holidays or do they give them up for American traditions?

How many immigrants don't like it here and return to their country?

How does the U.S. decide who can come to this country and who can't? Have these laws changed over the years? Should they be changed again?

Should anyone who wants to come here be allowed to come?

Should refugees from all the wars, in Haiti, Bosnia, Serbia, and wherever else _all_ be allowed to enter the U.S.?

Should we have a national language and everyone have to speak English only?

What can schools and social agencies do to help people adjust to life in the U.S.?

available on the proposed topics. Now is the time to show your students how to take brief, two- or three-sentence notes on index cards, starting with noting the pertinent bibliographic information such as author's name, book or document title, illustrator, date of publication, publisher, and call number (see Figure 3-2). In this way, when children return to the library to conduct their research, they have an idea of how to proceed with collecting information. They will have a good head start and won't feel overwhelmed by the task.

Defining the Inquiry Problem

One of the most important things to do before students begin to conduct an inquiry search is to review with them the problem they are going to research. Too often children think they understand an assignment only to arrive at the media center unable to tell the media specialist what they are looking for. Therefore, carefully review with them what they will be do-

FIGURE 3-2 Sample Index Card

TITLE: Ellis Island   **CALL NO:** 325.1
AUTHOR: Leonard Everett Fisher
ILLUSTRATOR: old photographs
PUBLISHER: Holiday House   **DATE:** 1986

SPECIAL FEATURES:
> real photographs of immigrants and Ellis Island, some drawings by the author, map of New York harbor showing Ellis Island. Author's note on p. 64 telling his sources for the information.

NOTES:
> Contains many quotes from people who came through Ellis Island about how they felt. They are from people's journals and diaries years ago when they were immigrants. The author writes about laws Congress passed telling who could enter the United States and how many people from each country could come here. He tells why these quotas were set.

---

ing and why they need to do it. Using Fisher's *Ellis Island* as an example, review the book's final pages, which discuss early immigration laws and the imposition of national quotas for immigration. These pages can be a basis for defining the research problem, making sure that students understand the problem and what the goals are for their inquiry searches.

Another book that could be used to help define the problem to be researched is *Immigration: How Should It Be Controlled?* by Meish Goldish (1994, 21st Century Books). This thought-provoking volume, after presenting a brief overview of the history of U.S. immigration, discusses the effects of immigration policies in this century and what language and economic problems have resulted. The book encourages children to think about immigration from a global perspective.

Another title that looks at immigration from a microscopic perspective but which can be universalized to all immigrant groups is Dorothy and Thomas Hoobler's *The Italian American Family Album* (1994, Oxford University Press). Here readers see why a specific group of immigrants came to America and how they made new lives for themselves, retaining some of the old ways and adapting them to new customs. Using first-person diaries, letters, and oral histories—always valuable resources for students doing research—this book personalizes the subject of immigration so that children can understand how this topic affects all of us.

Each of these books can be used to encourage children to write questions they want to answer while doing their research. Their questions should be written in their own journals and included in each group's listing of *What We Want to Know,* the second part of the *K-W-L* strategy. As children proceed through the inquiry process, it is not uncommon for them to continue to generate related questions they want answers to; these questions should be included on their *K-W-L* charts, where practical, and answered in the course of their research.

Evaluating the Parts of a Book

Before your students do any research, you should review the parts of a book with them, showing how to effectively use all the clues that are provided in the book's format and design. Using *Dougal Dixon's Dinosaurs* (1993, Boyds Mills Press) as an example, examine the title page, the reverse of the title page, table of contents, index, glossary, illustrations, chapter headings, charts, graphs, and any other information contained in the book as well as the book jacket. The jacket tells readers who the author is and the author's qualifications for writing the book. Point out to your students how important it is to try to verify an author's competence and integrity, that having this information allows them to have confidence that the material in the book is accurate. Direct your students to search for names of any professional authorities on the subject who may be acknowledged as contributors to or reviewers of the text, as further evidence of the book's accuracy. In this book, students will note that two widely acclaimed scientists are thanked on the back of the title page for their expert contributions; a listing of their qualifications is provided. Students will also see on the book jacket the endorsement of a scientific society, which is identified on the back of the title page. The society's address is provided in case readers want to write for more information.

Next, direct students to the table of contents page. Here they will see highly detailed chapter headings and subheadings. Students who want to use *Dinosaurs* (Dixon, 1993) for research will have a clear idea of the information it contains. The index is the next part of the book students should examine; it too describes topics and subtopics found in the book. A note explains that page numbers in bold type refer to illustrations and those in regular type to text, so children can go directly to the information they are seeking. Important features of a successful informational book are a glossary of scientific and technical terms and a listing of the sources used to obtain the book's illustrations. Both of these appear in *Dinosaurs,* making the book even more useful for young researchers. A section labeled "Do You Know" makes browsing more efficient because it highlights the text's salient information.

There are several other features to have children look for: clarity of illustrations and diagrams along with carefully labeled explanatory captions and the inclusion of charts, diagrams, maps, and time lines. Ask the children to look at these features to determine whether they complement and extend the text and if the labels are clear and easy to read. There are many features to examine that make Dixon's book "user friendly" and can serve as guidelines for evaluating informational books. Once children understand what to look for when selecting books, they will be more critical information consumers, better able to conduct effective information searches and to successfully access the information they need.

Now examine the text with your students. The author's voice can be heard expressing his knowledge and enthusiasm for the subject, unlike in textbooks, which in their effort to be objective express no point of view and appear to be written by faceless committees. In Dixon's book, as in any well-written informational trade book, readers can see that the author tries to distinguish between what is acknowledged fact and what is theory and speculation: phrases like "may have been" and "scientists think this is possible" appear throughout the text. The author also documents the facts he presents and cites his sources of information. When there is no clear answer, Dixon has the integrity to write, "We do not really know..." (p. 116). As in any good informational book, the author lets readers know where controversy exists in the professional community (we have underlined phrases for emphasis):

> Dinosaurs were reptiles, <u>and so it was always thought that they were cold-blooded</u>. <u>But in the 1970s some scientists began to think</u> that they may have actually been warm-blooded. <u>Evidence came from several points:</u> the way the dinosaurs stood—straight-legged like mammals; from their big rib cages that could have held mammal-like hearts and lungs; and from their bones that contained channels for fast blood circulation as in warm-blooded animals' bones. <u>Other scientists still regarded</u> dinosaurs as being cold-blooded. <u>They could not believe</u> that a big, long-necked, plant-eating dinosaur could possibly have eaten enough food to fuel a warm-blooded lifestyle. And their bodies were so massive that they would have been able to keep in their heat in cool weather.
>
> <u>More recent studies of dinosaur bones suggest</u>... (pp. 98–99)

It is important for children to be exposed to this type of writing; it helps them develop their critical-reading skills and learn how to evaluate materials for possible use in their own research. These qualities of informational trade books are important for children to consider when they evaluate books or other media sources to be selected and used in their research projects.

Accessing and Retrieving Resources

The next step in the inquiry process is to have the library media specialist demonstrate information-gathering strategies that your students will need when they are ready to search the library's book and media resources. In its publication *Information Power* (AASL, 1988) the American Association of School Librarians recommends that classroom teachers and school library media specialists work closely together to ensure that all resources of the media center are made available to students, along with instructions on their use. In fact, the guidelines proclaim it is the school librarian's "responsibility" (AASL, 1988, p. 29) to provide whatever guidance is necessary to students so that they can access, manipulate, and retrieve data stored in the various media center resources. While trade books still form the basis of most school library collections and will continue to do so for some time, the use of electronic print storage and retrieval systems is becoming increasingly common. Children need to know how to access and search the "information superhighway" if they are to be successful information users in their lifetimes. As more and more information is being stored on CD-ROM discs, they need to know how to access online communication systems, manipulate large databases, and search through information.

It is not unusual for students to need assistance in searching through the media center's resources. When contacted in advance, the library media specialist can prepare a demonstration of various search strategies to be used with the different media forms. In this way, children can learn to develop their own systematic, thorough searching procedures so they can effectively conduct an inquiry search through all the media systems available in the library media center. Minimally, they need to be shown how to search manually through a traditional card catalog, use standard and specialized reference works, and conduct a computer search of significant databases in order to complete a successful information search. Once they are able to manipulate physical access to information and ideas and have retrieved information they think will be useful to them in providing solutions to their inquiry searches, their evaluation skills, as previously described, become critically important.

Media centers have two distinct retrieval systems that children need to know how to use. A traditional retrieval system consists of a catalog in card or book form which directs users to open shelves where books in the circulating and reference collections are stored. An electronic retrieval system may include any of several state-of-the-art components. Your school media center may have its "card catalog" stored on a computer system; if this is the case, it is simply a matter of learning the corresponding computer commands and proceeding with a traditional catalog search. Many media centers provide access to the holdings of other libraries, and students may do computer searches to retrieve data from other libraries, academic sources, and public and private agencies. Many schools are now linked electronically via local area or long-distance networks, the "information super-highway" from which students can access and retrieve information. Online database searching of electronically stored data will provide students with much information they would not otherwise have access to. In this way, students can retrieve documents, journal articles, pages from specialized reference works, and other items not available in your school's media center. Your media specialist will know which electronic retrieval systems best suit your students' needs and will provide the necessary help to make them knowledgeable in using the appropriate systems.

Children need to be reminded frequently to note in their inquiry journals the sources they have consulted in their media searches in case they need to consult those sources again and to prepare a list of references they consulted while doing their information searches.

As children actively proceed with the information-gathering process, they need time to share and discuss, in small-group settings, the information they have retrieved. When students have found conflicting or incomplete information, suggestions will usually come from other group members to go back to the media center and search further. Because children initially have worked on their own, they will be able to recommend to each other research sources they have used and then work collaboratively in their small groups to find answers to questions the group has raised.

PROBLEM-SOLVING STRATEGIES

As children proceed through the initial stages of searching, selecting, accessing, and retrieving information while conducting an inquiry search, they need to learn analyzing and evaluating strategies and how to synthesize information into a meaningful framework so it can be shared with others. While many of these skills are usually taught at the middle and high school levels, through the use of trade books these strategies can be effectively demonstrated for elementary school children. Many trade books are available that can serve as models for children to use in the problem-solving phase of their inquiry searches. In this section we shall survey several titles and show how they serve as models for children to learn problem-solving strategies.

Once children have searched and retrieved books and other media they think will be useful in finding answers to the problem they are trying to solve, they are ready to closely examine the information and determine if it is suitable for their needs. First, students need to organize the books and media they have retrieved into some coherent order so they don't feel overwhelmed by a huge stack of material. At this point you might suggest they look at the questions they are trying to answer, then organize the books and media into piles corresponding to the various research questions. For instance, there are several books about eagles that children inquiring about this topic might retrieve. Remind children to use these techniques for browsing through a book: Inspect the book jacket, table of contents, index, chapter headings, and other parts of the book to get an idea of its contents.

Children might decide Dorothy Hinshaw Patent's *Where the Bald Eagles Gather* (1984, Clarion) should go in a pile with other books telling about eagles as an endangered species and about efforts to save them. It would be placed alongside Paula Hendrich's *Saving America's Birds* (1982, Lothrop, Lee & Shepard). Another book that would be placed there is Hope Ryden's *America's Bald Eagle* (1985, Putnam), which gives information about efforts to save the eagle across the United States.

Catskill Eagle (1991, Philomel), illustrated by Thomas Locker using Herman Melville's text, portrays the eagle soaring into the sky against the majesty of nature and should be put with books that depict the natural environment and habits of eagles. *The Book of Eagles* by Helen Roney Sattler (1989, Lothrop, Lee & Shepard) describes sixty different eagles in great detail, with maps and accurate illustrations of characteristics of many eagle species, and should be put with similarly classified books. Millicent Selsam and Joyce Hunt's book *A First Look at Owls, Eagles, and Other Hunters of the Sky* (1986, Walker) belongs with this group of books because of its emphasis on classification and its question-and-answer format about eagles and other birds.

While sorting the materials they have gathered might seem like a time-consuming step that may be omitted, it is important in the process of getting children to think critically about what they will do with the information they have retrieved and whether or not it is appropriate to their needs. If children learn to focus on answering questions that result from problems they are trying to solve, their thinking skills will be sharper and their final written presentations will address the subject with clarity and a meaningful response. They will be able to see for themselves the results of their own efforts.

ANALYZING AND EVALUATING INFORMATION

Your students are now ready to start the process of analyzing and evaluating the retrieved materials. Since many children find the idea of being a cowboy glamorous and exciting, a group of your students might choose to inquire about cowboys. They would want to know what cowboys' lives and work are really like, whether this lifestyle will survive into the future, and in what ways it can be expected to change. Let us compare and contrast the information in several recent titles about cowboys that your students might retrieve from the media center's book collection. They will be compared and contrasted in an attempt to evaluate the accuracy and reliability of their accounts of cowboy life and analyzed for their suitability in answering the proposed questions.

By tracing the career of one old-time cowboy, *Cowboy Country* by Ann Herbert Scott and illustrator Ted Lewin (1993, Clarion) offers children opportunities to explore in depth what a cowboy's life is like today and compare it with life in the past. Information in this book is conveyed equally through text and illustrations and is told in a narrative style similar to stories that young children are used to reading. Information is compiled from interviews with several older cowboys.

There is no index, table of contents, or bibliography. Instead, the note about the author found on the book jacket attests to the probable reliability of the information about past and present cowboy life. The Nevada Arts Council gave the author a grant to interview old cowboys, or "buckaroos" as they are called. Also, noting that the author lives in Nevada, readers can assume that she has some familiarity with the work and lifestyle of cowboys. The book jacket notes reveal that the artist prepared for doing the illustrations by taking "thousands of photographs" in northern Nevada.

These insights would seem to affirm the author's and artist's integrity in doing this book and therefore the reliability of its contents.

The text, related through an old cowboy's point of view, tells how life has changed since he first started working. The cowboy's enthusiasm for his work is clearly portrayed. He believes that, despite changes such as reliance on trucks as well as horses to do the work, every day is still an exciting challenge, and he would still choose to be a cowboy today. Because watercolors are used rather than photographs, the illustrator is able to capture the western scenes most of us associate with cowboys as well as the essence of contemporary western life.

In analyzing the text to see if it answers the questions being asked, readers can find many instances of the old-time cowboy explaining that the most important thing for a cowboy to know is the nature of the animals he works with and cares for, the cows themselves. He says that what people see depicted on television as the glamor of cowboy life, the bronco busting and fancy roping, is secondary to knowing how to take care of cows. He discusses survival of the cowboy lifestyle and what changes can be expected by talking about the increasing role of women in ranching, the influence of modern technology, and the need to be responsive to ever increasing government regulations.

A great deal of information is presented in this book in a style that is readily accessible to children in the middle grades. As children gain familiarity with different literary forms, they will be increasingly able to compare this book with other texts that have a more traditional informational style and format. They will be able to understand that *Cowboy Country,* despite its deceptive story book appearance, is a valid informational book that will be very useful in their effort to find out about cowboys' lives. An effective use of this book is to help children appreciate different literary styles and to offer them the possibility of preparing their own research in a form other than a standard piece of expository writing.

Remind your students as they go through the analysis and evaluation process to keep their index cards up to date. Every book title, author, publisher, and year of publication should be noted on a separate index card along with two or three sentences about the book. At the same time they should keep entering information on individual *K-W-L* charts in their journals so they can write their own responses to the inquiry questions. They should also contribute to the completion of the class's *K-W-L* chart. Encourage children to write their responses and answers to the inquiry questions using their own words. As children compare the texts of different trade books, they will realize that books on the same subject contain similar information. They will also understand that being an author means creating a text that says exactly what the author wants to say in the author's own words. When they are comfortable doing this, children will know that they are authors, too. They will write like authors and be more critical readers.

Another book children might retrieve as they search for books about cowboys is Brent Ashabranner's *Born to the Land* (1989, Putnam). This book follows a traditional informational style, with an index, table of contents, and bibliography making its information readily accessible to readers. The book offers a realistic portrait of ranch and farm life in a small community in New Mexico. Interviews with several community members provide descriptions about the daily life of cowboys, ranchers, and farmers, with their many joys and hardships. It does not gloss over the dangers cowboys face, both from natural and man-made sources, but it presents an optimistic outlook that this lifestyle will survive into the future. Illustrations are somber black-and-white photographs that reflect a realistic picture of cowboy life.

Children need to ask themselves if *Born to the Land* answers their questions about what cowboys' work is really like and whether or not cowboys will exist in the future. Using the evaluation techniques previously described, they can make a partial decision about this title's usefulness. Then they should compare this book with Scott's *Cowboy Country* to try to assess the accuracy and reliability of the information contained in the two books. In doing this, they would see that both books give some historical background about cowboys. Scott's book intersperses historical data along with current information about cowboy life today and speculation about what the future holds in store for working cowboys.

Ashabranner's book is organized in chapters starting with a historical perspective, so readers can find most of the historical information in one place. In Ashabranner's compare/contrast organization, expectations for the future of the cowboy lifestyle all appear in one chapter, except where the author interviews people on the basis of their ethnic background. This might present some difficulties for children who are looking for information arranged according to occupation. On the other hand, the book will be seen as reliable because it contains interviews with men and women, young and old people, and people of different colors and ethnic backgrounds. They all say that ranch and farm life is difficult and uncertain, but they all affirm their love for this lifestyle and say they would not give it up. If children are aware of different styles of expository writing, they will readily understand the compare/contrast organization of *Born to the Land*.

Ashabranner's book shows actual photographs of the subjects the author interviews, making the reading experi-

ence very realistic for young readers. They can point to a photograph of 17-year-old Justin Nunn and then read about his
life and activities in the text. Such realism gives the book a
stamp of authenticity; it tells readers that the information is
reliable because real people are telling about their own lives.
Elementary school children may possibly see Ann Scott's
Cowboy Country as a "story" because of its format and illustrations and conclude that stories are "made up" and not
"real." If this is their interpretation of the book, then the
book's information has to be seen as questionable in terms of
its accuracy and reliability. If, however, children can apply
the evaluation standards that you have explained to them,
they will see this book as highly useful, containing accurate
information that compares favorably with Ashabranner's
Born to the Land. They will recognize that both books provide answers to their questions.

Ranch Dressing: The Story of Western Wear by Jean M.
Greenlaw (1993, Dutton) is another book children might
retrieve as they continue their information searches. It contains many of the special features we tell children to look for
in informational books: an index and table of contents, bibliography and list of titles for suggested reading, photography
credits, and a list of museums to visit. A note about the
author gives her qualifications for writing the book and
explains her special interest in the subject. All of these features make the book highly useful to readers as they search
for information. They also help children evaluate the reliability of the text's information. The opening chapter tells the
history of cowboys and how the cowboy's uniquely American
character developed in response to geography, climate, and
the socio-historical setting. Greenlaw tries to look at what
changes can be expected in the future.

As readers would predict from the title, the book is primarily devoted to telling the story of western, or cowboy,

dress. According to the author, cowboy clothing styles developed in response to daily needs of cowboys as they went about their work of ranching and tending cattle. This provides a unique perspective on the nature of the cowboy lifestyle and the demands of the cowboy workplace. Children—and most adults—would not think of trying to describe an occupation according to how the workers dress for the job. Is the information in this book accurate? When compared with the other two titles, the information about cowboys does appear to be similar. Readers can conclude that Greenlaw's book is equally accurate. She also includes interviews with real cowboys and western wear manufacturers who recall interesting anecdotes that personalize the text and add to its believability.

The question still has to be asked: Is this book, despite its high interest level and the accuracy of its information, suitable for answering the children's proposed questions? Unlike Ashabranner's *Born to the Land,* where the book's organization enables children to lift answers directly out of the text without having to search for them, or Scott's *Cowboy Country,* where the entire text is a response to specific questions children are asking, *Ranch Dressing* presents answers to several of the inquiry questions, but in a form that does not make the answers immediately apparent. Children will not find answers to all their questions here, but they will find a great deal of information that is suitable to their needs and not available elsewhere. It is a very different perspective from what they are accustomed to, and one not available within the constraints of a textbook. If they read carefully, they will find unique details that will make their own final presentations much more interesting. There are unusual details here that grab the attention of readers and listeners, delighting them with unexpected facts. This is the sort of information that says the preparer was interested enough to search for little-known details and has taken the time to share them with readers. Indeed, children will have to read carefully and focus on finding information that answers the questions they are asking. But the effort will be well worth it.

These three books are typical of what children might retrieve as they search for answers to questions they propose on a given topic. The three authors' styles are very different from each other and the books need to be read carefully. Children need to become critical readers and thinkers to extract the information they need to answer their inquiry questions. They need to be sure of what questions they are really asking and be able to analyze and evaluate that information to be certain it is accurate and suitable for answering their questions. After reading the three books, children can generate a compare and contrast chart to visually display the information they have gleaned (see Figure 3-3).

The final step in the inquiry process is for children to take all the notes they have accumulated and synthesize them in their own thoughts and words into some form to share with others and to be read and reread.

FIGURE 3-3 Compare and Contrast Chart

Title/ Author	Provides Historical Background	Describes Current Lifestyle and Work	Predictions about Future Changes	Special Useful Features of the Book	How Information Was Compiled and Presented
Cowboy Country by Ann Scott	The old cowboy compares his job with his father's & grandfather's cowboy jobs. And he tells what he did when he was young.	Gives lots of details about what cowboys do, how hard they work in all weather, how many different subjects they have to know.	Tells about how computers and airplanes are used now on ranches, about new laws and women as cowboys.	No index, references, or bibliography. A note about how author & illus. got money to interview cowboys & take photos. It is easy to read, like a story.	Interviews with old-time cowboys. Author & illus. went to a ranch in Nevada. Presented as a story told to a young boy.
Born to the Land by Brent Ashabranner	Interviews with people who can remember what things were like long ago. Starts the book by telling about the community's history.	Lets the people he interviews describe their work & lives. Some things the author just tells, some things he asks detailed questions about.	Lets the people, ranchers, farmers, teenagers tell what they think the future will be. Retired people & teenagers think differently.	This reads more like a textbook. Has index, table of contents, bibliography. Photos show cowboys at work & with their families. Interviews with many people & teenagers.	Presented like people being interviewed in the newspaper or on TV. The author went to ranches and farms and lived with the people he writes about. Very realistic.
Ranch Dressing by Jean Greenlaw	Tells how cowboy clothes, hats, and boots developed because they were needed to do the work comfortably in all weather. Lots of unusual facts & details.	Describes how cowboys live and work by telling what they wear. Tells what different styles mean. Lots of interviews with real cowboys.	Tells some cowboy legends and why cowboys think their clothes will always be popular, why they'll always be heroes.	Has a list of cowboy museums to write or visit. Index, table of contents, bibliography, & list for further reading. Tells where photos come from. Tells why & how author wrote the book & checked the information.	Presented through interviews with real working cowboys and clothing manufacturers. Some are big companies & some are individual people. Did research at museums.

▶ 4

Informational Books and Content Area Writing

People write for many different purposes: to inform, to entertain, to persuade, to direct, to share ideas, to express personal feelings. In elementary classrooms, children write in all content areas, often referred to as "writing across the curriculum." In this chapter we discuss the different kinds or genres of writing and various ways or formats for students to organize information for their writing. Informational books provide children wonderful models of these different genres of writing as well as the different formats for presenting and sharing information. Writers of informational books for children impart to readers their enthusiasm for the topic and their ability to communicate factual information in engaging, creative, and humorous ways. Skilled writers craft text which is rich in imagery and descriptive language generating interest in the topic among readers. The discussion that follows is not meant to be all-inclusive, because it focuses on factual, expository writing and does not include other genres that emphasize imaginative, narrative writing such as stories, folk tales, and fantasies.

DIFFERENT GENRES OF WRITING

Different kinds or genres of writing serve the many purposes we have for writing. In this section we describe various genres of writing that convey factual information, and we highlight some informational books that provide models for the genres. When children compose, they must consider such elements as audience, style, tone, mood, word choice, and figurative language. In addition, when children write to share information, they may want to include some aids to further assist the reader: a glossary, table of contents, index, reference list, charts, maps, graphs, pictures, or diagrams. If their writing is the result of research and investigation, children should share with readers their references, which may include primary and secondary source material such as interviews, pamphlets, magazines, newspapers, letters, books, and diaries.

Autobiographies

An autobiography is an account of oneself—it gives children the opportunity to write about themselves, share personal experiences, and enhance their self-esteem as they recognize that they are important. Informational books show children how they can share information about themselves. In *Learning to Swim in Swaziland: A Child's-Eye View of a Southern African Country* (1993, Scholastic), 8-year-old Nila K. Leigh describes her new life in Swaziland. The book is printed in the child's own handwriting and includes her drawings and illustrations as well as a few photographs. Nila gives us information about Swaziland, going to school, recipes, and a Swazi folk tale.

Another way to share information about yourself is found in *Arctic Memories* (1988, Holt) by Normee Ekoomiak. This bilingual text (Inuktitut and English) is organized in short, one-page vignettes with accompanying illustrations that describe an aspect of Inuit life such as "In the Iglu" or "Playing on a Snowbank." Children could write books about themselves using the vignette structure as a guide. This format also lends itself well to collaborative class writing, in which each child individually or with a partner could contribute a page to a book about the class or school.

Biographies

Children learn about famous people as they engage in theme studies and content area work. They also can find out about the lives of people close to them: grandparents, parents, neighbors, siblings, or peers. Biographies for children of all ages abound and serve as solid writing models for them.

Younger children can consult the series of picture book biographies by David Adler. In *A Picture Book of Rosa Parks* (1993, Holiday House), illustrated by Robert Casilla, Adler describes the life of Rosa Parks, whose courageous refusal to move to the back of the bus precipitated the 1955 year-long bus boycott in Montgomery, Alabama. Dance world great Alvin Ailey is featured in the picture book biography *Alvin Ailey* (1993, Hyperion) by Andrea Davis Pinkney. Color scratchboard illustrations by Brian Pinkney create the feeling of movement throughout the text.

Older children can also write in a picture book format. The beautiful biographies of Cleopatra (*Cleopatra,* 1994, Morrow), Charles Dickens (*Charles Dickens: The Man Who Had Great Expectations,* 1993, Morrow), and William Shakespeare (*Bard of Avon: The Story of William Shakespeare;* 1992, Morrow) were illustrated by Diane Stanley and written by Stanley and Peter Vennema. The text, clearly intended for older readers, is supported with full-color paintings that authentically recreate the subject's life and times.

For a biographical format that more closely corresponds to biographies for adults, older children can look to the works of Russell Freedman—*Lincoln: A Photobiography* (1987, Clarion), *The Wright Brothers: How They Invented the Airplane* (1991, Clarion), *Eleanor: A Life of Discovery* (1993, Clarion)—or Jean Fritz—*You Want Women to Vote, Lizzie Stanton?* (1995, Putnam), *Harriet Beecher Stowe and the Beecher Preachers* (1994, Putnam). In these biographies meticulous research combines with an interesting storyline to create a character whom the reader comes to know very well. These authors always list their references and often share author notes, an aid to readers that children could include in their own writing.

If small groups or the entire class is reading biographies or researching individuals who are connected to each other in some way, the children may want to compile a collected biography. Each child contributes a biographical sketch of the person whom she/he researched for inclusion in a class book. Kathleen Krull introduces us to twenty musicians in *Lives of the Musicians: Good Times, Bad Times...and What the Neighbors Thought* (1993, Harcourt Brace). The history of each musician's life is enlivened by unusual anecdotes and little-known facts. For instance, we learn that Bach "loved food and coffee (once he wrote a whole cantata about coffee)" (p. 17). Another fine collection of biographical sketches based on interviews is *Talking with Artists* (1992, Bradbury) compiled and edited by Pat Cummings. This book uses an interview format to profile fourteen famous children's illustrators and serves as a good model for how to collect interview information.

Compare and Contrast

We often ask children to think about the similarities and differences that exist between concepts, topics, ideas, or books. In compare and contrast essays, students apply thinking skills to examine, clarify, and describe how things are alike and different. For example, in learning about the holiday Kwanzaa, students can read *Celebrating Kwanzaa* (1993, Holiday House) by Diane Hoyt-Goldsmith and *Seven Candles for Kwanzaa* (1993, Dial) by Andrea Davis Pinkney. The pairing of these two books for discussing and writing would work well for a teacher-led experience or for collaborative writing. After students discuss similarities and differences in the books' format and content, they can write about them. For instance, they may write that in *Celebrating Kwanzaa* the illustrations are color photographs taken by Lawrence Migdale, while in *Seven Candles for Kwanzaa* the illustrations by Brian Pinkney are painted scratchboard. Or they can discuss the similar ideas that are presented, such as what each day of Kwanzaa means.

Patricia and Fredrick McKissack's *Christmas in the Big House, Christmas in the Quarters* (1994, Scholastic) provides a fascinating model of compare and contrast writing. Set on a Virginia plantation in 1859, the book compares and contrasts the preparations for and celebration of Christmas in the plantation house with that of the slaves in their quarters. For example, while the family in the big house eats a Christmas dinner of roast turkey, mutton, ham and venison steaks, and bread pudding, the slaves are feasting on roast chicken, chitlings, possum, sweet potatoes, and ashcake.

Directions

Children demonstrate their understanding of a concept or a task by explaining it to someone else. Giving directions requires children to assume the perspective of their audience, anticipating what their audience will need to know to successfully complete the task. In writing directions for someone else to follow, children must use clear language presented in a logical sequence. In addition, children may want to supplement their written directions with graphic illustrations. In *Copier Creations* (1993, HarperCollins), Paul Fleischman gives instructions for children to assist them in using copy machines to make stationery, silhouettes, miniatures, jigsaw puzzles, and other items. The clear, step-by-step directions are supported by illustrations that further clarify the text. Directions to play a game are found in *Hopscotch Around the World* (1992, Morrow) by Mary D. Lankford, in which we learn how to play nineteen variations of hopscotch. The directions for each variant are accompanied by the hopscotch pattern to be drawn where the game will be played.

Experiment Reports

Students conduct experiments and hands-on activities in elementary science and need clear, effective models to guide them in writing-up their experiments. When children recount experiments, they must include specific elements, logical sequencing, and perhaps specialized vocabulary. Models of experiment writing are found in *Fun Machines: Step-by-Step Science Activity Projects from the Smithsonian Institution* (1993, Gareth Stevens), *Science Express: 50 Scientific Stunts from the Ontario Science Centre* (Gold, 1991, Addison-Wesley), and *Light Action! Amazing Experiments with Optics* (1993, HarperCollins) by Vicki Cobb and Josh Cobb. Each of these books follows the format for writing experiments including a statement of the experiment's purpose, the materials and equipment, the procedures to follow, and an explanation of what happened.

Interviews

Another type of writing is the interview. Students may interview adults in the community, family members, or their peers for a variety of purposes. If they are studying their community, students may interview community members and workers about the history, services provided, or other aspects of community life. If they are examining a current social or political issue, they may ask individuals for their opinion. Informational books show children how to take information given orally in an interview and write it in a way that maintains the interviewees' ideas and feelings. In *Freedom's Children: Young Civil Rights Activists Tell Their Own Stories* (1993, Putnam), author Ellen Levine expertly weaves together interviews with adults who as children and teenagers were involved in the civil rights movement of the 1950s and 1960s.

Howard Greenfeld interviewed adults who were hidden from the Nazis during World War II to write his book *Hidden Children* (1993, Ticknor & Fields). Greenfeld skillfully explains the context of World War II and combines excerpts from the interviews with biographical information about the hidden children. To indicate the distinction between biographical and historical information and the interviews themselves, interview material is printed in italics.

Journals

Children write in journals for many purposes. They may keep personal journals that reflect on their thoughts and feelings. Readers learn how an 11-year-old girl's life changes when war ravages her city in *Zlata's Diary: A Child's Life in Sarajevo* (1994, Viking) by Zlata Filiopovic.

Another kind of journal, a response journal, gives children an outlet for responding to books that they have read.

At times, children may assume the role of someone else when writing a journal. For example, in response to a book, children may assume the main character's role and keep a journal entry as that character. Or, if students are studying pioneer life, they may write a journal from the perspective of someone traveling in a covered wagon. A fine book to share as an example is *The Way West: Journal of a Pioneer Woman* (1993, Simon and Schuster) by Amelia Stewart Knight, with illustrations by Michael McCurdy. Mrs. Knight left Iowa in 1853 with her husband and seven children and ventured to the Oregon Territory. Her diary conveys the thoughts of a woman who never became famous, thereby reinforcing for children the value of keeping a journal as a way to chronicle their own lives and the fact that everyone has something worthwhile to say.

Students may also refer to journals of famous individuals who kept diaries to gain a valuable historical perspective on the individuals and to learn about their accomplishments and the times in which they lived. Peter and Connie Roop have edited the journals of several famous individuals. In *Off the Map: The Journals of Lewis and Clark* (1993, Walker) we learn that President Jefferson had instructed Lewis and Clark to keep diaries of their expedition. Now, over 150 years later, we can glimpse first-hand the thoughts and actions of these two famous explorers. We learn, for example, that on June 16, 1804, "Mosquitoes and ticks are exceedingly troublesome" (p. 6).

Letters

Children write letters for many authentic reasons: thank-you notes to guest speakers and other individuals, requests for information, communications to pen pals from another school or country. In *Dear Mr. Blueberry* (1991, Macmillan) by Simon James a fictional young girl conducts a correspondence about whales with the fictional Mr. Blueberry. In another picture book that contains much information about the West, *Kate Heads West* (1990, Bradbury) by Pat Brisson, Kate travels west with her friend Lucy and Lucy's mother. Her letters home to her friends and family convey factual information about the places she visits. An actual pen pal letter is found in *Siobhan's Journey: A Belfast Girl Visits the United States* (1993, Carolrhoda Books) by Barbara Beirne. The handwritten letter of Lauren Farrell, the American girl whose family will host Siobhan for a summer, is included and referred to in the book. Both business and personal letters of Abraham Lincoln are featured in *Lincoln: In His Own Words* (1993, Harcourt Brace) by Milton Meltzer. Through these letters Lincoln's honesty is revealed as he writes to a client whom he feels overpaid him for legal work. Loreen Leedy's *Messages in the Mailbox: How to Write a Letter* (1991, Holiday House) provides children with models for many kinds of letters including friendly letters, thank-you notes, get-well letters, and business letters.

Math Problems

Children daily encounter problems that require them to apply mathematical reasoning and skills. They need experience formulating these problems in writing. *Sideways Arithmetic from Wayside School* (1989, Scholastic) by Louis Sachar poses various mathematical word problems within a school context. For example, ten friends at recess are deciding whether to play freeze tag or basketball. Sachar notes each child's preference, such as Maurecia prefers "basketball, so long as there are five per team" while Jenny chooses "basketball, unless seven others want to play freeze tag" (p. 34). He then sets forth problems that require children to apply the preference information, such as "How many people played freeze tag and how many played basketball?" (p. 36).

For primary-age children, examples of addition and subtraction word problems are presented around the content of sea creatures in *Sea Sums* (1996, Hyperion) by Joy N. Hulme.

Newspapers

Newspapers are filled with many kinds of writing such as editorials, news stories, human interest stories, sports information, advertisements, and cartoons. Children can create a class newspaper that focuses on topics and themes under study or which serves as a news medium for the school or class itself. *The Furry News: How to Make a Newspaper* by Loreen Leedy (1990, Holiday House) and *Extra! Extra! The Who, What, Where, When and Why of Newspapers* (1994, Orchard) by Linda Granfield give children essential information about writing and publishing a class newspaper. In *Extra! Extra!,* examples of different types of newspaper articles are included such as news stories, sports and entertainment articles, and editorials. News stories from 1928 to 1988 can be found in *Weekly Reader: 60 Years of News for Kids, 1928–1988* (1988, World Almanac). In this book, children find models of news and feature stories from *Weekly Reader* since its inception. They learn about America's smallest pony in 1929; the opening of the world's highest building, the Empire State Building, in 1931; and how TV will affect the 1952 elections. These stories are solid models for the children's own newspaper articles.

Poetry

Poetry can convey information and present facts in an original and interesting way. Children may enjoy writing poems as a means of commenting on knowledge or insights. Bradford Hansen-Smith presents geometric concepts through rhymed verse in *The Hands-On Marvelous Ball Book* (1995, Scientific American Books). He describes:

> Hovering above the ground,
> The pattern slowly turned around.
> The six points moved one way,
> The centers another,
> Making two forms—
> One part of the other.
> The tetrahedron, a red form,
> The octahedron, a green.
> The difference between the forms
> In two colors could be seen. (p. 13)

As we know, poetry does not need to rhyme; many fine examples of unrhymed poetry are available. In *A Kettle of Hawks and Other Wildlife Groups* (1990, Lothrop, Lee & Shepard), Jim Arnosky describes six animal groups with a poem, each followed by expository text. For instance, he writes:

> A Swarm of Bees
> Bees in a ball—
> humming, buzzing,
> resting on a limb, then flying again,
> following their queen to begin a new hive.
> A Swarm of Bees in the orchard. (u.p.; by permission of William Morrow and Company, Inc.)

Following the poem, Arnosky provides a further explanation of how bees live in a group, using expository writing.

Children will identify with Opal, whose diary is written in free verse lyrical poetry in *Only Opal: The Diary of a Young Girl* by Opal Whiteley (1994, Philomel). Children learn about life in a lumber camp in the early 1900s revealed through the young girl's thoughts and feelings.

Postcards

A postcard enables children to convey a small amount of information in one paragraph. This genre can be used when studying various states, regions, or countries as children recount specific facts about the place being studied. In *Postcards from France* (1996, Steck-Vaughn) by Helen Arnold, children write postcards about France. Each postcard is illustrated with a color photograph of its content, such as the Eiffel Tower, the River Seine, or a food store in Brittany. In *Postcards from Pluto: A Tour of the Solar System* by Loreen Leedy (1993, Holiday House) a group of fictional children take a tour of the solar system. They write postcards to family and friends that describe each planet.

Recipes

Everyone loves to eat, and cooking is a classroom activity that motivates students and satisfies the palate. Cooking also has strong connections to content study and requires children to read and follow directions, measure, increase their vocabulary, and see science at work as ingredients change form from solids, liquids, and gases. If children are studying other cultures, they can create cookbooks of recipes. If family is being studied, they can collect favorite family recipes and compile them into an individual or class book. If a historical time period is being investigated, children can recreate dishes eaten in that time period. For instance, you can consult Lucille Recht Penner's *Eating the Plates: A Pilgrim Book of Food and Manners* (1991, Macmillan) to find recipes from the Pilgrims.

Many children's cookbooks are available. In *The Fairy Tale Cookbook* (1982, Macmillan), Carol MacGregor links the study of folk/fairy tales with cooking. She includes recipes for "Strega Nona's Magic Pasta," the "French Soldiers' Beef

Stew" (from *Stone Soup*), and "Rumpelstiltskin's Banana Bread." When you study plants, you may refer to Jean Craighead George's *The Wild, Wild Cookbook: A Guide for Young Wild-Food Foragers* (1982, Crowell), which describes wild plants and recipes with the primary ingredients of dandelions, cattails, acorns, and sunflower seeds. If you are doing an author study of Laura Ingalls Wilder or a theme on the pioneers, you may consult *The Little House Cookbook: Frontier Foods from Laura Ingalls Wilder's Classic Stories* (1979, HarperCollins) by Barbara Walker for recipes to prepare. In this book we find recipes for foods mentioned in the "Little House" books, such as corn dodgers, baked beans, and light biscuits.

Riddles and Jokes

Children always enjoy riddles and jokes, and writing them can be connected to content area learning and theme studies. Individually or in small groups, children can create riddles centered on the theme or topic of study. What an enjoyable way for children to share with each other the knowledge they have gained, increase their vocabulary, and become actively involved in word study! *Batty Riddles* (1993, Dial) by Kay Hall and Lisa Eisenberg centers on jokes about bats. Jokes include: "What famous flying mammal lived in ancient Egypt? Cleobatra!" (p. 13) or "What bat invaded Europe? Battilla the Hun!" (p. 21). Riddles that specifically reinforce language study can be written. Marvin Terban helps children clarify the concept of homographs in *The Dove Dove: Funny Homograph Riddles* (1988, Clarion). Riddles about colonial times and the American Revolution are found in *Remember Betsy Floss and other Colonial American Riddles* (1987, Holiday House) by David Adler. Here we learn "Why did the Pilgrims bring two drums and a saxophone on the Mayflower? They wanted to see Plymouth Rock" (u.p.).

DIFFERENT FORMATS FOR SHARING INFORMATION

As children inquire, explore, and examine the world around them, they want to share what they have learned with others. In addition to writing in different genres, children also organize information to be written in different formats. When they are engaged in theme studies and content area learning, children gather facts, quotes, ideas, and other materials. In order to share this information with others, they must organize and synthesize it in some way to effectively communicate their knowledge to an audience. We can provide children with models of informational books that show them varied formats for writing and the many interesting and innovative ways to organize and present information. Children can write individually or collaboratively with a partner.

ABC *Books*

When children have accumulated much information about a topic, they may wish to organize it according to an *ABC* format. This type of alphabet book gives them an easy way to organize and to focus on key vocabulary or items that reflect the topic. Each letter represents a word that is expanded upon and explained in a paragraph. For example, in *Illuminations* (1989, Bradbury) by Jonathan Hunt each letter of the alphabet represents an aspect of the Middle Ages, such as Illuminated manuscript (*I*) or troubadour (*T*). The Caldecott Award–winning *Ashanti to Zulu: African Traditions* (1976, Dial) by Margaret Musgrove, illustrated by Leo and Diane Dillon, introduces us to a distinct African tribe with each letter of the alphabet. In *Turtle Island ABC: A Gathering of Native American Symbols* (1994, HarperCollins), Gerald Hausman explains various aspects of Native American culture from Arrow and Buffalo to Pueblo and Turtle Island.

Annotated Catalogs

In an annotated catalog, children take a topic such as dinosaurs and write a description or explanation of specific classifications of the topic. These descriptions often are accompanied by an illustration. In *The Book of Eagles* (1989, Lothrop, Lee & Shepard), Helen Roney Sattler describes more than seventy-five kinds of eagles, each kind illustrated with a watercolor painting by Jean Zallinger. Similarly, Mary Barrett Brown discusses twenty-one water birds in text and watercolor illustration in *Wings Along the Waterway* (1992, Orchard). In another example, *The World of Animals* (1993, Viking), Desmond Morris presents written sketches of various animals including the elephant, koala, chimpanzee, and kangaroo. The annotated catalog lends itself well to group writing when the class or small groups are studying similar topics. Each child can individually research one smaller example of the larger category and write one part of a class compilation. The catalog also reinforces the thinking skill of categorizing as children see the relationships between a superordinate category and its component subcategories.

Chronological Organization

Often the nature of the information that has been gathered lends itself well to a chronological organization; the material is discussed in the order in which it occurred. In *Across America on an Emigrant Train* (1993, Clarion), Jim Murphy describes the journey of writer Robert Louis Stevenson by boat from Scotland to New York and then by train from New York to California in search of his true love.

Another fine example of a book organized chronologically is *Children of the Dust Bowl: The True Story of the School at Weedpatch Camp* (1992, Crown) by Jerry Stanley. Here we trace the journey of the "Okies" from Oklahoma to California during the Depression and learn how educator Leo Hart and "Okie" children built their own school at Weedpatch Camp. Their story is inspiring to students.

The sequence of the seasons is the framework in *The Reasons for the Seasons* (1995, Holiday House) by Gail Gibbons. This informational picture book explains the seasons to primary-age children.

Comic Strips (Cartoon Dialog)

Children enjoy reading the comics. The "bubble" dialog found in comic strips can be applied in children's writing as they create dialog to convey facts. This technique is used in the "Magic School Bus" series by Joanna Cole and Bruce Degen (*The Magic School Bus Inside a Hurricane,* 1995, Scholastic; *The Magic School Bus in the Time of the Dinosaurs,* 1994, Scholastic; etc.), in which children in Ms. Frizzle's class share vital information with readers in cartoon dialog. In *Take Action: An Environmental Book for Kids* (1992, Morrow), Ann Love and Jane Drake create cartoon dialog in which animals give information about the rain forest.

Conceptual Organization

Another way to organize information is by the main ideas or concepts that are being examined. Diane Swanson takes us on a *Safari Beneath the Sea* (1994, Sierra Club Books) as she arranges the book according to "Plants of Plenty," "Far-Out Fish," and "Mind-Boggling Mammals." In *Looking at Penguins* (1993, Holiday House), Dorothy Hinshaw Patent describes penguins by writing chapters on key ideas such as "Kinds of Penguins," "The Emperor," or "The Threatened Penguin." George Sullivan introduces children to the world of in-line skating in chapters that explain different aspects of skating, such as "How to Stop," "Swizzling," and "Sidesurfing"

(*In-Line Skating: A Complete Guide for Beginners,* 1993, Cobblehill).

Counting Books

A counting book, like an *ABC* book, need not be limited to reinforcing simple counting with young children. Jim Haskins has applied the number book format to present information about various countries in his "Count Your Way Through..." series. For example, in *Count Your Way Through India* (1989, Carolrhoda Books), Haskins illustrates each number with an item from Indian culture and includes a pronunciation guide. The reader counts one banyan tree; two circles on the flag of India; four tall towers, called minarets, at each corner of the Taj Mahal; and so on. Similarly, in *Count Your Way Through Korea* (1989, Carolrhoda Books), we learn about two Koreas, North and South; six gold medals at the 1984 Summer Olympic Games; and eight kinds of seasonings likely to be found at a Korean meal. Betsy Bowen uses the counting format in *Gathering: A Northwoods Counting Book* (1995, Little Brown), in which painted woodblock prints support textual information about Minnesota. For example, for the number 6, bags of wild rice, we learn that "wild rice is called mahnomin by the Ojibwe people here. They honor it as a gift to them from the Creator."

Informational Picture Books

In an informational picture book the illustrations and text work together to convey information. Children enjoy creating these kinds of books, in which illustrations may be their own drawings in various media, pictures from magazines, or any other type of illustration. Aliki's beautiful watercolor illustrations bring an aquarium to life in *My Visit to the Aquarium*

(1993, HarperCollins). Gail Gibbons recreates tropical rain forests in full-color illustrations done with watercolors, colored pencils, and India ink in *Nature's Green Umbrella: Tropical Rain Forests* (1994, Morrow).

If the class is studying a theme, children can contribute to a class book that collects their individual investigations. The class book can be formatted to include two pages for each child's work, one with the text and the other with an illustration provided by the child. For instance, in *O Canada* (1993, Ticknor & Fields) by Ted Harrison, each page describes one of Canada's provinces or territories such as Prince Edward Island, New Brunswick, and Quebec and is illustrated with a painting by the author.

Photo Essays

In a photo essay, photographs enhance the text and are essential to clearly conveying information. George Ancona introduces us to Don Ricardo, a Mexican craftsman known for "beautiful and unusual piñatas" (*The Piñata Maker,* 1994, Harcourt Brace). Through the text and color photographs we learn how he creates piñatas in a Mexican village. Jan Reynolds helps us travel around the world in photo essays about children in her "Vanishing Cultures" series. In *Mongolia* (1994, Harcourt Brace) we meet Dawa and Olana on the "great plains of Mongolia," as color photographs bring these Mongolian children to us. Primary-age children will delight in seeing through color photographs how mozzarella cheese is made in *Extra Cheese, Please: Mozzarella's Journey from Cow to Pizza* (1994, Boyds Mills Press) by Cris Peterson. National Geographic photographer Jim Brandenburg allows us to visit the Namib desert of southwest Africa, where the mystery of the desert and its plants, animals, and peoples are depicted in magnificent color photographs (*Sand and Fog: Adventures in Southern Africa,* 1994, Walker). Teachers have guided children to create photo essays by encouraging them to use their own cameras, by buying a class camera that the children can share, or by receiving special grants to purchase individual disposable cameras that enable each child to have a camera to create a photo essay on a self-selected topic.

Questions and Answers

A question/answer format can be used to share information. In this format a question is posed and then answered. In *Can You Guess?* (1993, Greenwillow), Margaret Miller adopts such a format in a beginning concept book illustrated with color photographs. She poses such questions as "What do you comb in the morning?" "What do you give to your dog?" or "What do you put on your head?" This format would be especially appropriate with beginning writers since it does not need to involve extensive text and helps them to clearly establish their purpose for writing. Seymour Simon uses a question/answer format in *New Questions and Answers about Dinosaurs* (1990, Morrow). In this book, Simon poses a specific question about dinosaurs that the text then answers. Examples of questions include "What are dinosaurs?" "Did the dinosaurs have families?" "Why did the dinosaurs become extinct?" You may refer to an article by Zarnowski (1991) in which she elaborates ways for children to apply a question/answer format in their own writing.

Scripts

Children enjoy acting out plays. A play script enables children to organize material they have learned on a topic into a form that they can then perform for others. Actor Ossie Davis has written a play for children about Frederick Douglass's life (*Escape to Freedom: A Play about Young Frederick Douglass,* Viking, 1978). This play, first performed in New York City, serves as a solid model of the play format for children. In addition, the author includes a bibliography reinforcing the concept that the play's material was researched by the author.

As children engage in inquiry projects, theme studies, and content area learning, they will write in various genres to explain, give directions, describe, and inform. When children share in writing what they have learned with others, they may select from a range of formats to organize and convey ideas, facts, and concepts.

Informational Books in Integrated Themes of Study

The second-grade classroom hummed with activity as children constructed air pollution gauges and designed new uses for two pieces of trash. Later in the day, children classified garbage items as recyclable, reusable, or reducible. The following day, children made recycled paper and wrote stories about "How I Can Make Every Day Earth Day." Books and magazines about ecology, pollution, and environmental issues spilled out of bookcases and children's desks. This group of second-graders was enthusiastically engaged in learning experiences supporting the theme, "It's the Only Earth We Have."

WHAT IS AN INTEGRATED THEME?

A theme of study provides children with opportunities to explore a topic, concept, or idea in an integrated and interconnected way. Conceptual development is emphasized as children discover the theme's interrelated elements in authentic and meaningful learning experiences. Student choice, inquiry, active participation, and higher-level thinking are essential. Reading, writing, speaking, listening, and visual experiences enable children to investigate, learn, and share. While specific content is learned, children are also engaged in the process of discovery.

A theme has several characteristics that distinguish it from traditional subject area study. Let's take one theme, "Hurricane," to exemplify these characteristics. First, a theme views content from an interrelated perspective rather than segmented into discrete subject areas. In the real world when we are interested in a topic, we don't ask whether this is science or social studies or math. Instead, we generate related questions that interest us and that we want answers for. Children, too, are curious to learn everything they can about a topic and do not compartmentalize their thinking into discrete content areas. Children's desire to explore a topic in depth will involve many subject areas. Themes build on students' interests and what they want to know about a topic from multiple perspectives.

A theme study also focuses on content knowledge and conceptual understanding, reading/writing, oral language, visual literacy, and applying thinking skills in meaningful ways. During the summer of 1992 several very large hurricanes pummeled Florida and Hawaii, generating much devastation as well as a great deal of interest among children and teachers about this natural phenomenon. Elementary teachers in one of our graduate classes during the fall of 1992 brainstormed a list of questions they or children might want to investigate. These questions could be categorized into subtopics or concepts as follows:

Weather

What causes hurricanes?

Is there a difference in the severity of hurricanes?

How do meteorologists know if a hurricane is coming?

How do you plot hurricanes on weather maps?

Geography/Location

Where do hurricanes usually occur?

What kinds of climate/locations support the formation of hurricanes?

How do hurricanes travel? Is there a general pattern to their movement?

History

What are some famous hurricanes in history?

What is the history of hurricanes in the United States?

How many hurricane-related deaths have occurred in the United States?

Why are hurricanes named the way they are?

Effects

What is the effect of hurricanes on the environment?
What happens to the water supply?

What happens to animals? Can they be left homeless?

What is the impact of hurricanes on peoples' lives in terms of homes, businesses, emotional trauma?

What is the effect of hurricanes on the local, state, and national economy?

Survival

How do people prepare for hurricane survival? Hurricane drills? Evacuation plans?

What types of assistance and relief efforts are made available to hurricane survivors?

What is the role of the Red Cross?

These questions would involve students with the content areas of math, science, social studies, the arts, and language arts as they actively investigate answers to them. But one theme may not necessarily integrate all content areas. Some disagreement exists regarding the terminology surrounding themes. Altwerger and Flores (1994) prefer the term *theme cycle* rather than *theme unit* to "reflect the recursive and spiraling process of knowledge construction" (p. 4). Regie Routman (1991) cautions that:

> Many of the thematic units teachers buy and create are nothing more than suggested activities clustered around a central focus or topic. The units incorporate some elements of math, science, social studies, art and music, but there is often little or no development of important ideas. This is correlation, not integration. (p. 277)

We shall use the broad term *theme study* to suggest a more flexible, recursive, and integrative interpretation of this type of curricular organization.

A second characteristic of a theme is that it provides children with choice. The students' role in a theme cycle has been described by Altwerger and Flores (1994) as follows:

> In the theme cycle, the students are involved in the entire process of theme development from deciding on topics, to planning learning experiences, gathering materials, researching information, and presenting what was learned. Students work in collaboration with the teacher as well as with each other in order to learn how to learn. (p. 4)

If a theme study has been initiated by the teacher, students still can have a choice as they generate the kinds of learning experiences that are possible and as they select the specific learning experiences they will pursue. They can share in choosing topics to explore in more depth, whether they will work in pairs or small groups, and what books they will read.

In theme work all children will not be engaged in the same activity at the same time. Children will assist in planning and directing the theme's development, which empowers all learners regardless of reading level or prior academic success.

Third, in a theme study, instruction is organized fluidly and flexibly. Children may work on some activities and experiences as a whole class, but they will also be working with a partner, in small groups, and by themselves. Instruction may be teacher-guided or student-initiated. Some topics lend themselves to mini-themes lasting from three days to one week, while other theme studies are longer, lasting typically from one month to six weeks. Subject time distinctions, such as 40 minutes for science, no longer exist as children actively pursue their theme-related activities. The day itself becomes more integrated as separate content boundaries blend together.

Fourth, diverse resources are used to support the theme. Children's books, magazines, resource people, field trips, media, and "realia" are some of the most commonly used resources. Informational books play an essential role in theme work since they provide important content and conceptual knowledge and also pique student interest. Informational books about the theme may be written on a range of reading levels, thus supporting children's individual needs.

We have been asked by teachers, "How do I decide on a theme?" "How do I get started?" A theme may originate from your students' interests, a timely event (such as a hurricane), or required topics from courses of study in your school district or state. As you begin to think about a theme, you may want to take the list of brainstormed questions and then create a web, a visual representation of possible learning experiences and resources to develop concepts, content, and processes involved in the theme. It is often advantageous to generate these possibilities with the children or with your colleagues. After the teachers had generated their questions about hurricanes, they then created a web of initial possibilities of ideas (Figure 5-1).

What are some specific ways that informational books support theme studies? Informational books or excerpts from them can be read aloud by teachers to introduce the theme or to share specific important facts of interest. An informational book may also serve as an impetus for development of the theme itself. A child may read a book or a teacher may read one aloud that arouses curiosity and initiates a theme. For example, the book *Flight: The Journey of Charles Lindbergh* (1991, Philomel) by Robert Burleigh, with its suspenseful tone, powerful language, and magnificent paintings by Mike Wimmer, may stimulate a theme on aviation. Informational books may also be used by children for research and investigation or simply be read for pleasure and to satisfy an interest or curiosity. Throughout a theme study informational books integrate with learning experiences in writing, content area reading, oral language, visual literacy, and thinking skills.

Let's look at three themes: "To the Top of the World: The Arctic Region of North America" for primary children, "A House Divided: America's Civil War Period" for grades 4–6; and "Constructions" for grades 3–5 to explore some specific ideas that incorporate informational books. The discussion of these themes will focus specifically on the role of informational books and therefore should not be considered all-inclusive of the learning possibilities for each theme.

TO THE TOP OF THE WORLD

The theme "To the Top of the World: The Arctic Region of North America" borrows its title from the informational picture book *To the Top of The World: Adventures with Arctic Wolves* (1993, Walker) by National Geographic photographer

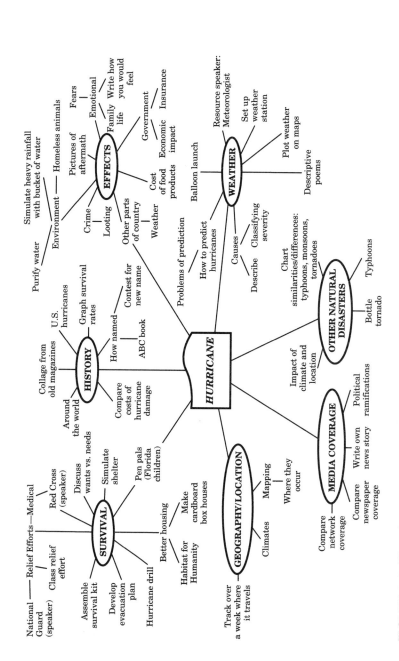

FIGURE 5-1 Hurricane Web

115

Jim Brandenburg. It has been developed for children in grades 1–3. To introduce the Arctic to young children, the teacher may read aloud the informational picture book *Arctic Summer* by Downs Matthews (1993, Simon and Schuster), which would effectively set the stage for a fascinating theme study. The book begins:

> Far to the north lies a part of the Earth called the Arctic. Winters there are long and hard. Years ago, native people in the Arctic thought of winter as a great giant made of frost. When the giant came down from the north, all living things found places to hide. The giant would lie down on the land and it would freeze. He would sleep and the world would become dark and cold. Only the polar bears would walk around. (u.p.)

This book, with beautiful full-color photographs by Dan Guravich, visually introduces children to the Arctic region. For a companion book, the teacher can then read the cumulative informational text *Here Is the Arctic Winter* by Madeleine Dunphy (1993, Hyperion), illustrated with paintings by Alan Robinson. After reading these books, children may generate questions they have about the Arctic such as:

> Why does the sun sometimes shine day and night and other times it doesn't shine at all?
> What kinds of plants live in the Arctic?
> How are lemmings like mice or other animals? Do lemmings live in Ohio or Maine or Texas?
> What is the difference between a fox and a wolf?
> What animals live in the Arctic?
> How cold is it in the Arctic? How much snow falls each year?
> What kinds of animals live in the Arctic sea?
> Who lives in the Arctic? What kind of houses do they live in? What do they eat? Do children there go to school?

Based on the children's questions, the teacher may add to the web of possibilities that she has created (Figure 5-2).

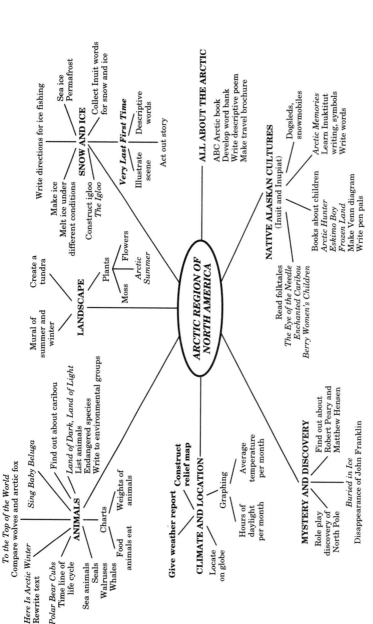

FIGURE 5-2 Arctic Web

117

A study of the Arctic will involve vocabulary growth as children learn names of plants and animals and specialized terms that relate specifically to this region. One way to record new vocabulary is through class and individual word banks. A class word bank may be generated as new words are introduced through the books that are read. The teacher or children may write these words on chart paper that hangs in the room to become a word wall that children refer to in their writing and oral discussions. Children may also choose to develop their own individual word banks that they keep for personal use. This may take the form of index cards or an "Arctic dictionary." Some words that will most likely be included in their word banks are *igloo, Inuit, ptarmigan, caribou, tundra,* and *sea ice.* In the Inuit language there are many different words for ice and snow. In *Arctic Hunter* by Diane Hoyt-Goldsmith (1992, Holiday House) we learn from Reggie, the Inupiat Eskimo boy narrator, that "by its color and texture, I can tell if the ice is thick and strong, or rotting and weak" (p. 18). The teacher can begin a separate chart listing the new ice and snow words and their specialized meaning.

Illustrations in many of the books for young children are color photographs, which provide a pre-reading opportunity to view the visuals for information and to engage in meaningful discussion about what the photographs show, the detail involved, and how to predict what the text might be about. In *Frozen Land* by Jan Reynolds (1993, Harcourt Brace), children meet Kenalogak, a young Inuit girl. Through color photographs and text the Inuit's daily life becomes visible and children gain information about Inuit clothing, ice formations, and tools. Directions for building an igloo are made clear by photographs. Children could work in small groups to create a life-size igloo for the class out of blocks or large cardboard boxes, or miniature, individual igloos with sugar cubes or marshmallows. To support this project, the teacher might share a book intended for older children, *The Igloo* by Charlotte and David Yue (1988, Houghton Mifflin), which includes a diagram of both the igloo's interior and exterior. Although children cannot independently read *The Igloo,* it gives information in both text and illustrations relevant to the project. Through teacher guidance this information becomes accessible to younger children.

Primary-grade children can begin to develop research skills as they investigate the Arctic's climate, land, and people and seek answers to the questions they have generated. As children read books about the Arctic, they may want to record what they are learning in a variety of ways. Such recording helps reinforce the content learned, encourages children to see connections among various ideas, and enhances comprehension. For example, as children are reading *Polar Bear Cubs* by Downs Matthews (1989, Simon and Schuster), they can develop a time line chronicling the life cycle of the bear cubs. The book begins in April when "the bears mate" and continues to September when the female bear "leaves the sea ice and returns to her birthplace" and to December when she "gives birth to her cubs." Then the book sequentially describes the life of the young bear cubs. Through a time line the sequence of events becomes clearer to children as they read with the purpose of understanding this life cycle.

Another way of recording information is by a Venn diagram, which enables children to visually see similarities and differences. Several books focus on the daily lives of Inuit children: *Arctic Hunter* by Diane Hoyt-Goldsmith (1992, Holiday House), *Frozen Land: Vanishing Cultures* by Jan Reynolds (1993, Harcourt Brace), and *Eskimo Boy* by Russ Kendall (1992, Scholastic). As students read these books, they can complete a Venn diagram to illustrate the similarities and differences between the Inuit children and themselves (Figure 5-3). Children can also reflect on what life would be like as an Inuit child by writing a journal entry.

An Arctic region theme also gives children opportunities to apply their math skills. For instance, it would be interesting to graph the number of times various animals are discussed in the books being read. Before beginning the theme, the teacher might ask the class which animals they associate with the Arctic region. As books are read, a tally could be kept to indicate the number of animals mentioned in each book. Students could then transfer their tally to a graph. Once the graph has been constructed, various questions can be asked and answered, such as, "Which animal is mentioned most often?" "Are animals mentioned most often the same ones mentioned by the children at the start of the theme?" Other information about animals may be compared in graph form, such as their weight or what they eat. Another graph may focus on the average temperature during different months of the year and compare Arctic temperatures with those in various regions of the United States, including the children's own community.

Children are intrigued by mystery and adventure. A study of the Arctic includes the mystery of Sir John Franklin, who led an expedition from England in 1845 to find the Northwest Passage and disappeared. With teacher guidance, children will enjoy hearing about this famous expedition in *Buried in Ice: The Mystery of a Lost Arctic Expedition* by Owen Beattie and John Geiger (1992, Scholastic). Although written for older children, the book includes all kinds of illustrations and maps and excerpts that can be read aloud by the teacher.

A HOUSE DIVIDED: AMERICA'S CIVIL WAR PERIOD

In the Civil War theme developed for grades 4–6, the teacher wanted to emphasize the following concepts: the system of

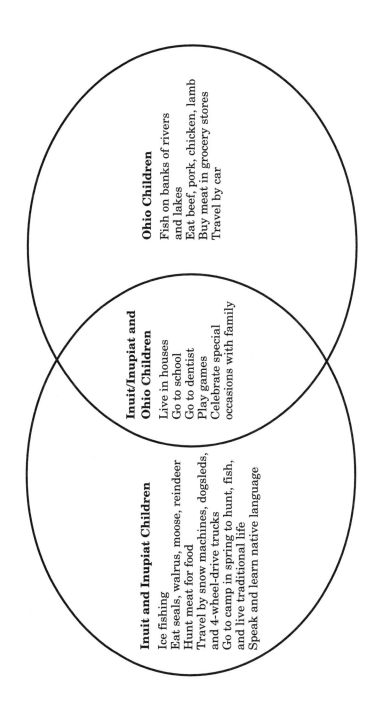

Inuit and Inupiat Children

Ice fishing
Eat seals, walrus, moose, reindeer
Hunt meat for food
Travel by snow machines, dogsleds, and 4-wheel-drive trucks
Go to camp in spring to hunt, fish, and live traditional life
Speak and learn native language

Inuit/Inupiat and Ohio Children

Live in houses
Go to school
Go to dentist
Play games
Celebrate special occasions with family

Ohio Children

Fish on banks of rivers and lakes
Eat beef, pork, chicken, lamb
Buy meat in grocery stores
Travel by car

FIGURE 5-3 Venn Diagram

slavery, causes of the Civil War, major military events of the war, leadership roles of important figures, changes in the concepts of equality, and the aftermath of the war (its legacy for our time). Because this theme related to required course of study content, the teacher initially created a web of possibilities to guide her (Figure 5-4).

One section of the web centers on the Underground Railroad, which the teacher introduces by reading aloud to the class the picture book *Sweet Clara and the Freedom Quilt* (1993, Knopf) by Debra Hopkinson and illustrated by James Ransome. Students with interest in the Underground Railroad may want to investigate further individually or in a group and read *Get on Board: The Story of the Underground Railroad* (1993, Scholastic) by Jim Haskins, which gives them a comprehensive explanation of the Underground Railroad. Here they will find a map of the escape routes that will guide them in constructing their own map of a specific route or of the entire system. They will find out how songs and spirituals carried double meanings and clues for the slaves. In the song "Follow the Drinking Gourd" are directions for following the Underground Railroad. Students may consult the picture book version of the song, *Follow the Drinking Gourd* (1988, Knopf) by Jeannette Winter, and listen to a recording of the song. They may also share the song and its meaning with the entire class. Haskins introduces famous runaway slaves such as Harriet Tubman, Josiah Henson, and Eliza Harris. Students may then refer to Virginia Hamilton's *Many Thousand Gone: African Americans from Slavery to Freedom* (1993, Knopf) to learn more about these courageous individuals. They may want to create short dramas about runaway slaves that they would perform.

Another learning opportunity for children is to compare and contrast fiction and nonfiction accounts of historic events

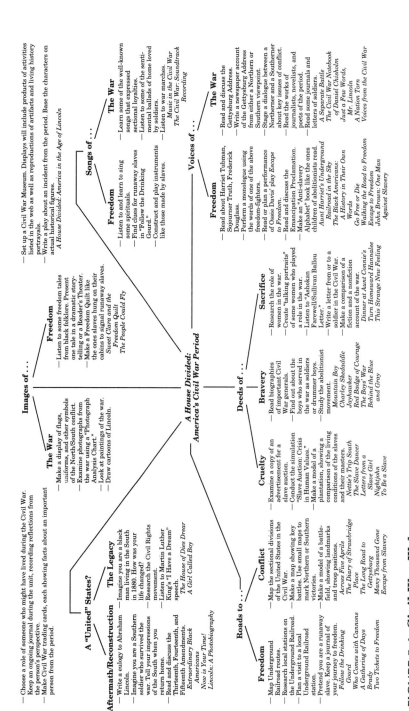

FIGURE 5-4 Civil War Web

123

and real and imaginary historical figures. Students will enjoy reading *Letters from a Slave Girl: The Story of Harriet Jacobs* (1992, Scribner's) by Mary Lyons, which provides a fictional set of letters based on the actual life of Harriet Jacobs, a slave who lived from 1813–1897. Students can then compare and contrast these letters and reflections to actual accounts of former slaves presented in the Newbery Honor book *To Be a Slave* (1968, Dial) by Julius Lester. Students may demonstrate these comparisons in various ways: a comparative chart, a Venn diagram, oral discussion, or a written compare/contrast essay. Students may wish to discuss differences in tone, style, and information. They may also comment on which version they preferred and why.

Students may also compare and contrast two versions of the same incident or the life of an individual. For instance, they may read *Two Tickets to Freedom: The True Story of Ellen and William Craft, Fugitive Slaves* by Florence Freedman (1971, Simon and Schuster) and also the account of the Crafts' escape in *Escape from Slavery: Five Journeys to Freedom* by Doreen Rappaport (1991, HarperCollins). This slave couple's exciting escape would lend itself well to reader's theater, a dramatic interpretation similar to a radio program in which an expressive oral rendition is presented without scenery or costumes. After students have delineated similarities and differences in the versions, they can create a reader's theater script and present the play to the entire class. Or students may wish to assume a fugitive slave's perspective and write a story of their own escape to freedom. Their narrative may include the starting and ending points, hiding places, possible routes, methods of travel, and individuals who provided assistance. Instead of a story, students may compose a poem as a more personal response to the escape of slaves. Poems about slavery and the Civil War can be found in *Followers of the North Star: Rhymes about African American*

Heroes, Heroines and Historical Times by Susan Altman and Susan Lechner (1993, Children's Press).

Informational books on the Civil War provide a fine vehicle to enhance visual literacy. In *The Long Road to Gettysburg* (1992, Clarion) by Jim Murphy many maps detail the Gettysburg campaign. Each of the maps shows a visual representation of different stages of the battle. Students learn about scale and can use the scale to measure the miles traveled by Lee's army or Stuart's cavalry. Students also interpret the map key and various symbols that indicate the route of Lee's army or the approach of Union reinforcements. Students view how mountains, lakes, and rivers are depicted on the map and locate major cities and towns. They see the difference between the map of the Gettysburg campaign (p. 26) that shows Pennsylvania, Maryland, and Virginia and the map that shows the detail of the Gettysburg battlefield itself (p. 75). After reading these maps and discussing them, students may design their own map of some aspect of the advancing soldiers or the battleground itself drawn to scale.

A variety of visuals are found in *A Separate Battle: Women and the Civil War* (1991, Lodestar) by Ina Chang. Chang includes a page of picture credits that indicates the sources for the book's illustrations and photographs. Paintings, portraits, and old photographs enhance and extend the text. Students can discuss the different types of illustrations, comparing and contrasting them as well as personally responding to them. One picture illustrates the code used by a Confederate spy. Students may want to hypothesize how to decipher this code. Another illustration depicts a publicity sign for a lecture by Clara Barton. Students may analyze the information contained in the sign and compare it to present-day advertisements for lectures and entertainments. Do they contain the same information? Are they formatted similarly? What techniques are used to arouse audience interest? An

1869 political cartoon is critical of the women's rights movement. After carefully inspecting the cartoon, students may explain its meaning and discuss its relevance to the world today. What do current political cartoons satirize?

This theme lends itself to the important skill of perspective taking. Many books include varied points of view about the war. In *The Long Road to Gettysburg,* children learn the viewpoints of two participants in the battle, a 19-year-old Confederate lieutenant and a 17-year-old Union soldier. This factual account of the war can be compared with multiple perspectives on the Battle of Bull Run provided in *Bull Run* (1993, HarperCollins), a historical fiction work by Paul Fleischman. Children may identify with one of the characters in either book or create a new character and assume that identity as they write, debate, or dramatically portray differing points of view.

A Civil War study incorporates many math applications. A wealth of statistics can be collected as books are read. In *Till Victory Is Won: Black Soldiers in the Civil War* by Zak Mettger (1994, Lodestar) we learn that 200,000 black men fought and almost 39,000 died during the Civil War. We also find out that while black soldiers were paid $10 per month of which $3 was deducted for clothing, their white counterparts were paid $16 per month. Other comparisons can be made dealing with the number of losses per battle or the number of soldiers in the Confederate and Union armies.

Informational books also are a motivating and interesting source for children to learn how to locate information, utilize a book's various parts, and construct meaning. The role of the table of contents, index, glossary, chapter headings, and subheadings can be explained in a meaningful context as children are actively engaged in reading the book. The fascinating account of boys 16 years old or younger who fought in the Civil War, *The Boys' War* by Jim Murphy (1990, Houghton Mifflin), features chapters with intriguing titles that arouse curiosity, such as "Prison Bars and the Surgeon's Stew" or "What a Foolish Boy." The book includes an index as well as a bibliography and acknowledgments, thus modeling for children the key components of a solidly researched piece. Strategies in reading expository text can also be enhanced as students learn to look for certain key words and patterns to assist them in constructing meaning.

CONSTRUCTIONS

"Constructions," a theme designed for children in grades 3–5, integrates the study of geometry and measurement with other areas such as architecture, careers, history, and culture. This theme lends itself well to students pursuing their own interests and specific projects. The sample web in Figure 5-5 indicates some of the possibilities for this theme.

Children may begin their study by walking through their neighborhood to observe shapes and parts of buildings such as doorways and windows. Observations may be recorded to document the types of shapes and frequency of their occurrence as Steven T. Johnson does in his Caldecott Honor book, *Alphabet City* (Viking, 1995). *Let There Be Light: A Book about Windows* (1988, Crowell) can be consulted to learn why windows come in different shapes and what purposes windows have served throughout history. For instance, readers become aware of patterns in glass to form stained-glass windows for churches and cathedrals and dormer windows set in the roofs of French castles. Children can examine the color photographs of famous doors and windows and describe their varied shapes in *Round Buildings, Square Buildings, & Buildings That Wiggle Like a Fish* (1988, Knopf) by Philip M. Isaacson. They see the famous Flatiron Building in Manhattan, which is shaped "like a thin wedge.... It is so narrow that its two long sides almost

Measure It!

Draw floor plan of your bedroom.
Make scale drawing of classroom.
Chalk out measurements of Mayflower on playground; how many students fit?
Sketch blueprint of dream house.

Shapes Galore!

Take neighborhood walk.
Record observations.
Draw pictures of doors and windows.
Build a model pyramid.
Design stained-glass window.
Write different perspectives on pyramid construction (pharaoh, architect, workers).

The Village of Round & Square Houses
Let There Be Light
Round Buildings, Square Buildings & Buildings That Wiggle Like a Fish
Pyramid
An Egyptian Pyramid
Alphabet City

Changes in Constructions

Choose timeframe and place; design exterior of house.
Write—who built Stonehenge and why?
Create construction of the future.
Develop time line of famous historical constructions.

The Great Wall of China
Stonehenge

CONSTRUCTIONS

People Who Construct

Make biographical profiles of famous architects (Frank Lloyd Wright).
Keep an architect's journal through a building's construction.
Generate list of occupations.
Hear guest speakers from community.

Architects Make Zig Zags
Cutters, Carvers and the Cathedral
Let's Build a House

What's It Made Of?

Observe material samples.
Write descriptive poem about materials.
Compare/contrast building materials.
Make pretzel cabin.
Grow grass roof for sod house.
Create dwelling from materials in your environment.

Building
Houses
Sod Houses on the Great Plains
Frontier Home

Kinds of Constructions

Visit a skyscraper.
Process drama on castle renovation.
Construct freestanding tower with pins and straws.
Build skyscraper.
Create own original structure.

A Skyscraper Story
The Skyscraper Book
Cross-Section Castle
Super Structures

FIGURE 5-5 Construction Web

come to a point" (p. 22). Isaacson describes buildings with unusual shapes such as the TWA terminal at JFK International Airport in New York, which has "soft, flowing shapes" and "looks as though it is sailing through air" (p. 39).

A famous shape associated with structures is the pyramid. Several books describe the ancient Egyptian pyramids and their construction. *An Egyptian Pyramid* (1991, Peter Bedrick Books) by Jacqueline Morley, Mark Bergin, and John James and *Pyramid* (1975, Houghton Mifflin) by David Macaulay reveal the long, laborious process of building a pyramid. After reading these books, children may build a model pyramid. They may also want to write about the pyramid's construction from varied viewpoints such as the architect who designed it, a worker involved in building it, or the pharaoh for whom it was being built.

Children are intrigued by certain types of buildings such as castles and skyscrapers. Some children may wish to examine the construction of these buildings in more depth. In *A Skyscraper Story* (1990, Carolrhoda Books), author Charlotte Wilcox explains that "the story of the skyscraper is an American story because the skyscraper was born in America" (p. 9) and, further, that "two features make a building a skyscraper. To be a skyscraper, a building must be very tall. Most modern skyscrapers are 20 to 70 stories high.... A skyscraper must also be built around a frame made of steel, or steel and concrete" (p. 10). By tracing the construction of one skyscraper, the Norwest Center in Minneapolis, Wilcox shows the importance of applying mathematical concepts to a real situation. Readers learn about blueprints, dead load, live load, and wind load. A section of the "shopping list" details the amount of materials needed to construct the building such as "16,500 tons of steel, 6 tons of screws, and 7 acres of stone (enough to cover 64 basketball courts)" (p. 18).

Children can also refer to James Cross Giblin's *The Skyscraper Book* (1981, Crowell) for a history of the skyscraper, a description of different styles of skyscrapers, and mathematical information on construction. After generating specific questions about skyscrapers, children can visit a local skyscraper and list ideas for constructing their own skyscraper. In pairs or small groups, children can plan, design, and construct a skyscraper from materials that they have selected. Or they can see how tall a tower they can construct using only pins and straws.

Children may choose to investigate the construction of castles in more depth. David Macaulay's *Castle* (1977, Houghton Mifflin) and Stephen Biesty's *Cross-Sections Castle* (1994, Dorling Kindersley) provide comprehensive views of the construction of castles. The importance of different shapes is revealed by Biesty, who points out, for example, the need for arrow loops to allow archers to fire their arrows at the enemies while remaining protected themselves. The various shapes of these slits are carefully illustrated, and children could design their own arrow loops or other kinds of structures that could be used for protection. In the Macaulay book a floor plan of the castle maps out its sections and their relationship to each other. Students may use this book as a basis for a process drama experience in which they assume the roles of historical society members involved in restoring an old castle to its original state so it can be visited by tourists. Students would determine all the tasks that need to be done, the required materials, and the cost of various aspects of the renovation. The book's glossary and illustrations of various types of workers will assist students in this learning experience.

People who construct is another area to be investigated as children explore careers involved in construction. Parents

and community members can serve as valuable resource people for this aspect of the theme by visiting the classroom to
share what they do. George Ancona describes many types of
occupations involved in constructing a cathedral in the photo
essay *Cutters, Carvers and the Cathedral* (1995, Lothrop,
Lee & Shepard). Color photographs show the stone carver at
work with his chisel and mallet; saw runners who operate
the diamond-tipped saw that cuts limestone blocks; and the
chief masonry draftsman, who says that "to be a good mason,
you must have a good sense of geometry." Occupations are
also highlighted in *Let's Build a House: A White Cottage
Before Winter* (1990, Ideals) by Russ Flint, in which we learn
about the well driller, building inspector, and masons.
Children can generate a comprehensive list of various types
of workers and then individually or in pairs write an *ABC*
book about the occupations involved in construction.
Children can also investigate and write biographical profiles
of famous architects such as Frank Lloyd Wright.

Super Structures (1996, Dorling Kindersley) by Philip
Wilkinson prompts students to brainstorm all kinds of structures. How are such structures as theaters, sewers, tunnels,
bridges, and roller coasters constructed and how do they
work? Students could choose a structure of interest to them
and create their own model of it. Or they may construct an
original structure such as a maze or an imaginary structure
that they have invented.

Another area to pursue focuses on the different materials used in various constructions. Philip Wilkinson identifies many materials in *Building* (1995, Dorling Kindersley),
such as earth, bricks, stone, and wood. Samples of these
materials can be brought into class for children to observe
and compare regarding their weight, texture, and durabili-
ty. Samples of other materials such as stucco and marble

can also be included. Books describe specific materials, such as how prairie sod was used to build houses on the Great Plains in *Sod Houses on the Great Plains* (1995, Holiday House) by Glenn Rounds. Raymond Bial details the materials used in building a log cabin in *Frontier Home* (1993, Houghton Mifflin). Piero Ventura traces the history of dwellings and the materials used to build them in *Houses* (1993, Houghton Mifflin). Here readers learn about caves; pile dwellings; and building with stone, bricks, reinforced concrete, and iron. After reading these books, children may create a dwelling out of various materials such as making a cabin of pretzels, forming a grass roof for a sod home, or collecting unusual items in the community and using them to construct a dwelling.

Students can also reflect on changes in construction by learning about famous constructions of the past or imagining structures of the future. Books such as *The Great Wall of China* (1986, Macmillan) by Leonard Everett Fisher and *Stonehenge* (1989, Greenhaven) by Peter and Connie Roop introduce children to ancient structures that have survived. After reading the book about Stonehenge, children can speculate by writing their own theories about who built Stonehenge and why. They can also project into the future and describe a construction for a distant time. Throughout this theme, children will be applying their understanding of measurement as they draw floor plans, generate blueprints, and construct scale models.

SUMMARY

This chapter has described a sampling of the kinds of learning experiences possible for children as they explore a theme through informational books. The possibilities are limitless as teachers and children generate ideas to investigate about a theme in more depth. Informational books are rich in content, both in text and illustrations, and successfully support children's learning across the content areas as well as the acquisition of reading, writing, oral language, visual literacy, and thinking skills.

References

Altwerger, B., and Flores, B. 1994. Theme cycles: Creating communities of learners. *Primary Voices K–6, 2,* 2–6.

American Association of School Librarians (AASL). 1988. *Information power: Guidelines for school library media programs.* Chicago: American Library Association.

Armbruster, B. 1984. The problem of inconsiderate text. In G. Duffy, L. Roehler, and J. Mason (Eds.), *Comprehension and instruction.* New York: Longman.

Armento, B. J., Nash, G. B., Salter, C. L., and Wixon, K. K. 1991. *This Is My Country* (4th-grade social studies textbook). Boston: Houghton Mifflin.

Barrow, L. H. 1990. Elementary science textbooks and potential magnet misconceptions. *School Science and Mathematics, 90* (8), 716–720.

Beck, I. L., and McKeown, M. G. 1991. Social studies texts are hard to understand: Mediating some of the difficulties. *Language Arts, 68* (6), 482–490.

Beck, I.L., McKeown, M. G., and Gromell, E. W. 1989. Learning from social studies texts. *Cognition and Instruction, 6,* 99–158.

Bernstein, H. T. 1985. The new politics of textbook adoption. *Phi Delta Kappan, 66* (7), 463–466.

Bissex, G. 1980. *GNYS AT WRK: A child learns to read and write.* Cambridge, MA: Harvard University Press.

Bosma, B. 1992. The voice of learning: Teacher, child, and text. In E. B. Freeman and D. G. Person (Eds.), *Using nonfiction trade books in the elementary classroom* (pp. 46–54). Urbana, IL: National Council of Teachers of English.

Britton, B. K., Gulgoz, S., and Glynn, S. 1993. Impact of good and poor writing on learners: Research and theory. In B. K. Britton, A. Woodward, and M. Binkley (Eds.), *Learning from textbooks: Theory and practice* (pp. 1–46). Hillsdale, NJ: Lawrence Erlbaum.

Calkins, L. 1986. *The art of teaching writing.* Portsmouth, NH: Heinemann.

Carter, B., and Abrahamson, R. F. 1993. Factual history: Nonfiction in the social studies program. In B. E. Cullinan (Ed.), *Fact and fiction: Literature across the curriculum* (pp. 31–56). Newark, DE: International Reading Association.

Chall, J. S., and Conrad, S. S. 1991. *Should textbooks challenge students? The case for easier or harder books.* New York: Teachers College Press.

Christie, F. 1987. Factual writing in the first years of school. *Australian Journal of Reading, 10* (4), 207–216.

Cohen, H., and Staley, F. 1982. Integrating with science: One way to bring science back into the elementary day. *School Science and Mathematics, 82* (7), 565–572.

Cohn, D., and Wendt, S. J. 1993. Literature adds up for math class. In B. E. Cullinan (Ed.), *Fact and fiction: Literature across the curriculum* (pp. 57–67). Newark, DE: International Reading Association.

Cox, B., Shanahan, T., and Tinzmann, M. B. 1991. Children's knowledge of organization, cohesion, and voice in written exposition. *Research in the Teaching of English, 25,* 179–218.

Crook, P. R., and Lehman, B. A. 1990. On track with trade books. *Science and Children, 27,* 22–23.

Cullinan, B. 1989. Latching on to literature: Reading initiatives take hold. *School Library Journal, 35* (8), 27–31.

Davidson, N. 1990. *Cooperative learning in mathematics: A handbook for teachers.* New York: Addison-Wesley.

Deford, D. E. 1981. Literacy: Reading, writing and other essentials. *Language Arts, 58,* 652–658.

Dewey, J. 1938. *Experience and education.* New York: Macmillan.

Eckhoff, B. 1983. How reading affects children's writing. *Language Arts, 60,* 607–616.

Edwards, N., and Richey, H. G. 1963. *The school in the American social order.* Boston: Houghton Mifflin.

Ennis, R. H. 1985. Goals for a critical thinking curriculum. In A. Costa (Ed.), *Developing minds: A resource book for teaching thinking* (pp. 54–57). Alexandria, VA: Association for Supervision and Curriculum Development.

Ennis, R. H. 1987. A taxonomy of critical thinking dispositions and abilities. In J. Baron and R. Sternberg (Eds.), *Teaching thinking skills: Theory and practice.* New York: Freeman.

Finley, F. N. 1991. Why students have trouble learning from science texts. In C. M. Santa and D.E. Alvermann (Eds.), *Science learning: Processes and applications* (pp. 22–27). Newark, DE: International Reading Association.

Fogarty, R. 1991. Ten ways to integrate curriculum. *Educational Leadership, 49* (2), 61–65.

Frank, M. S. 1992. On the road to literacy: Pathways through science trade books. In E. B. Freeman and D. G. Person (Eds.), *Using nonfiction trade books in the elementary classroom* (pp. 55–64). Urbana, IL: National Council of Teachers of English.

Freedman, R. 1992. Fact or fiction? In E. B. Freeman and D. G. Person (Eds.), *Using nonfiction trade books in the elementary classroom* (pp. 2–10). Urbana, IL: National Council of Teachers of English.

Freeman, E. B. 1991. Informational books: Models for student report writing. *Language Arts, 68* (6), 470–473.

Galda, L., and Cullinan, B. E. 1991. Literature for literacy: What research says about the benefits of using trade books in the classroom. In J. Flood, J. M. Jensen, D. Lapp, and J. R. Squire (Eds.), *Handbook of research on teaching the English language arts* (pp. 529–535). New York: Macmillan.

Graves, D. 1983. *Writing: Teachers and children at work.* Portsmouth, NH: Heinemann.

Greene, L. C. 1991. Science-centered curriculum in elementary school. *Educational Leadership, 49* (2), 42–46.

Gunning, T. G. 1992. *Creative reading instruction for all children.* Boston: Allyn and Bacon.

Halliday, M. A. K. 1975. *Learning how to mean: Exploration in the development of language.* London: Edward Arnold.

Hammack, D. C. 1990. *U.S. history report card: The achievement of fourth-, eighth-, and twelfth-grade students in 1988; Trends from 1986 to 1988 in the factual knowledge of high school juniors.* Washington, DC: U.S. Department of Education, Office of Education Research and Information.

Hansen, J. 1987. *When writers read.* Portsmouth, NH: Heinemann.

Hiebert, E. H. 1991. Research directions: Department editor's note. *Language Arts, 68,* 482.

Holliday, W. G. 1991. Helping students learn effectively from science text. In C. M. Santa and D. E. Alvermann (Eds.), *Science learning: Processes and applications* (pp. 38–47). Newark, DE: International Reading Association.

Irwin, J. W., and Baker, I. 1989. *Promoting active reading comprehension strategies.* Englewood Cliffs, NJ: Prentice-Hall.

Kent, C. E. 1984. A linguist compares narrative and expository prose. *Journal of Reading, 28,* 232–236.

Kleiman, G. M. 1991. Mathematics across the curriculum. *Educational Leadership, 49* (2), 48–51.

Langer, J. 1986. *Children reading and writing: Structures and strategies.* Norwood, NJ: Ablex.

Lapp, D., and Flood, J. 1993. Literature in the science program. In B. E. Cullinan (Ed.), *Fact or fiction: Literature across the curriculum* (pp. 68–79). Newark, DE: International Reading Association.

Levstik, L. S. 1990. Research currents: Mediating content through literary texts. *Language Arts, 67,* 848–853.

Mechling, K. R., and Kepler, L. 1991. Start with science. *Instructor, 100,* 35–38.

Meltzer, M. 1993. Voices from the past. In M. O. Tunnell and R. Ammon (Eds.), *The story of ourselves: Teaching history through children's literature* (pp. 27–30). Portsmouth, NH: Heinemann.

Meyer, L. A. 1991. Are science textbooks considerate? In C. M. Santa and D. E. Alvermann (Eds.), *Science learning: Processes and applications* (pp. 28–37). Newark, DE: International Reading Association.

Monson, R. J., and Monson, M. P. 1994. Literacy as inquiry: An interview with Jerome C. Harste. *The Reading Teacher, 47* (7), 518–521.

National Commission on Excellence in Education. 1983. *A nation at risk: The imperative for educational reform.* Washington, DC: Author.

National Council for the Social Studies (NCSS). 1993. *Curriculum standards for the social studies.* Washington, DC: Author.

National Council for the Social Studies (NCSS). 1994. *Expectations of excellence: Curriculum standards for social studies.* Washington, DC: Author.

National Council of Teachers of English. 1993. *Learning through language.* Pamphlet prepared by the Language and Learning Across the Curriculum Committee. Urbana, IL: Author.

National Council of Teachers of Mathematics (NCTM), Commission on Standards for School Mathematics. 1989. *Curriculum and evaluation standards for school mathematics.* Reston, VA: Author.

National Council of Teachers of Mathematics (NCTM), Commission on Teaching Standards for School Mathematics. 1991. *Professional standards for teaching mathematics.* Reston, VA: Author.

National Research Council. 1990. *Fulfilling the promise: Biology education in the nation's schools.* Washington, DC: National Academy Press.

National Research Council. 1994. *National science education standards: An enhanced sampler.* Washington, DC: National Academy of Sciences.

Newkirk, T. 1989. *More than stories: The range of children's writing.* Portsmouth, NH: Heineman.

Nordstrom, V. 1992. Reducing the text burden: Using children's literature and trade books in elementary school science education. *Reference Services Review,* Spring, 57–70.

Ogle, D. 1986. *K-W-L:* A teaching model that develops active reading of expository text. *The Reading Teacher, 39,* 564–570.

Pappas, C. C. 1991. Fostering full access to literacy by including information books. *Language Arts, 68,* 449–462.

Pappas, C. C. 1993. Is narrative primary? Some insights from kindergarteners' pretend readings of stories and information books. *Journal of Reading Behavior, 25* (1), 97–129.

Pearson, P. D., and Fielding, L. 1991. Comprehension instruction. In R. Barr, M. L. Kamil, P. Mosenthal, and P. D. Pearson (Eds.), *Handbook of reading research* (vol. 2). New York: Longman.

Peetom, A. 1993. Little children lead the way. In S. Tchudi (Ed.), *The astonishing curriculum: Integrating science and humanities through language* (pp. 1–10). Urbana, IL: National Council of Teachers of English.

Perrone, V. 1972. *Open education: Promise and problems.* Bloomington, IN: Phi Delta Kappa.

Person, D. G., and Cullinan, B. E. 1992. Windows through time: Literature of the social studies. In E. B. Freeman and D. G. Person (Eds.), *Using nonfiction trade books in the elementary classroom* (pp. 65–75). Urbana, IL: National Council of Teachers of English.

Piaget, J. 1970. Piaget's theory. In P. Mussen (Ed.), *Carmichael's manual of child psychology* (vol. 1) (pp. 703–732). New York: Wiley.

Raphael, T. E., Englert, C. S., and Kirschner, B. W. 1989. Acquisition of expository writing skills. In J. M. Mason (Ed.), *Reading and writing connections* (pp. 261–290). Boston: Allyn and Bacon.

Ravitch, D., and Finn, C. 1987. *What do our 17-year-olds know?* New York: HarperCollins.

Rosenblatt, L. 1991. Literature—S.O.S.! *Language Arts, 68,* 444–448.

Routman, R. 1991. *Invitations: Changing as teachers and learners K–12.* Portsmouth, NH: Heinemann.

Rumelhart, D. 1984. Understanding understanding. In J. Flood (Ed.), *Understanding reading comprehension* (pp. 1–20). Newark, DE: International Reading Association.

Rutherford, F. J., and Ahlgren, A. 1990. *Science for all Americans.* New York: Oxford University Press.

Ryan, F., and Ellis, A. 1974. *Instructional implications of inquiry.* Englewood Cliffs, NJ: Prentice-Hall.

Salesi, R. 1992. Reading and writing connection: Supporting content-area literacy through nonfiction trade books. In E. B. Freeman and D. G. Person (Eds.), *Using nonfiction trade books in the elementary class-*

room (pp. 86–94). Urbana, IL: National Council of Teachers of English.

Santa, C. M. and Alvermann, D. E. (Eds.). 1991. *Science learning: Processes and applications.* Newark, DE: International Reading Association.

Saul W., and Jagusch, S. A. 1991. *Vital connections: Children, science, and books.* Portsmouth, NH: Heinemann.

Scharer, P. L., Freeman, E. B., Lehman, B. A., and Allen, V. G. 1993. Literacy and literature in elementary classrooms: Teachers' beliefs and practices. In D. J. Leu and C. K. Kinzer (Eds.), *Examining central issues in literacy research, theory, and practice* (pp. 359–366). Chicago: National Reading Conference.

Sewall, G. 1988a. American history textbooks: Where do we go from here? *Phi Delta Kappan, 69* (8), 553–558.

Sewall, G. 1988b. Literacy lackluster: The unhappy state of American history textbooks. *American Educator, 12,* 32–37.

Silberman, C. (Ed.). 1973. *The open classroom reader.* New York: Random House.

Teale, W. H. 1984. Reading to young children: Its significance for literacy development. In H. Goelman, A. A. Oberg, and F. Smith (Eds.), *Awakening to literacy* (pp. 110–121). Portsmouth, NH: Heinemann.

Tyson-Bernstein, H. 1988. *A conspiracy of good intentions: America's textbook fiasco.* Washington, DC: Council for Basic Education.

Vygotsky, L. S. 1962. *Thought and language.* Cambridge, MA: MIT Press.

Whitin, D. J., and Wilde, S. 1992. *Read any good math lately? Children's books for mathematical learning, K–6.* Portsmouth, NH: Heinemann.

Wood, K. D. 1992. Fostering collaborative reading and writing experiences in mathematics. *Journal of Reading, 36* (2), 96–103.

Wood, T. L., and Wood, W. L. 1988. Assessing potential difficulties in comprehending fourth grade science textbooks. *Science Education, 72* (5), 561–574.

Woodward, A., and Elliott, D. L. 1990. Textbooks: Consensus and controversy. In D. L. Elliott and A. Woodward (Eds.), *Textbooks and schooling in the United States.* Chicago: National Society for the Study of Education.

Woodward, A., Elliott, D. L., and Nagel, K. C. 1986. Beyond textbooks in elementary social studies. *Social Education, 50* (1), 50–53.

Zarnowski, M. 1991. The question-and-answer book: A format for young historians. *Social Studies for the Young Learner, 4* (2), 5–7.

Children's Books Cited

Adler, David A. *Remember Betsy Floss and Other Colonial American Riddles.* Illustrated by John Wallner. New York: Holiday House, 1987. Brings funny smiles and silly giggles to middle-graders' faces as they learn American history in the context of humorous word play, puns, and picturesque metaphors.

Adler, David A. *A Picture Book of Rosa Parks.* Illustrated by Robert Casilla. New York: Holiday House, 1993. Details Rosa Parks's commitment to the civil rights movement and her pivotal role in the 1955 Montgomery bus boycott as well as the contributions of other civil rights activists.

Aliki. *My Visit to the Aquarium.* New York: HarperCollins, 1993. Brightly colored illustrations and photographs of aquarium exhibits and marine creatures draw young readers into sharing the underwater habitats of the aquarium residents. The illustrations depict a wide range of multicultural visitors and physical abilities.

Altman, Susan, and Susan Lechner. *Followers of the North Star: Rhymes about African American Heroes, Heroines, and Historical Times.* Illustrated by Byron Wooden. Chicago: Children's Press, 1993. The metaphor of the North Star pointing the way to freedom for African American slaves is used with a readily accessible rap musical style to tell the stories of those who risked their lives to gain freedom.

Ancona, George. *The Piñata Maker: El Piñatero.* San Diego, CA: Harcourt Brace, 1994. Through photos and text showing a day in the life of a kindly Mexican piñata maker, readers gain a sense of the warmth and caring among the villagers and a rich appreciation of Latino culture and customs.

Ancona, George. *Cutters, Carvers and the Cathedral.* New York: Lothrop, Lee & Shepard, 1995. This photo essay details the construction of the Cathedral of Saint John the Divine in New York City. Color photographs feature various occupations involved in building a cathedral from the quarry worker in Indiana to the draftsperson who produces templates for the blocks on the computer.

Arnold, Caroline. *Dinosaurs All Around: An Artist's View of the Prehistoric World.* Photographs by Richard Hewitt. New York: Clarion, 1993. The painstaking research done by scientists and artists is evident in the re-creation of prehistoric creatures based on careful study of fossil remains. The museum quality, life-size dinosaurs are as authentic as the latest research allows.

Arnold, Helen. *Postcards from France.* Austin, TX: Steck-Vaughn, 1996. Each double-page spread includes a postcard describing an aspect of France accompanied by a color photograph.

Arnosky, Jim. *A Kettle of Fish and Other Wildlife Groups.* New York: Lothrop, Lee & Shepard, 1990. A noted naturalist describes six different animal species who form themselves into groups and live together in the wild. Arnosky explains how living in a group contributes to an animal's ability to survive and protect itself.

Ashabranner, Brent. *Born to the Land: An American Portrait.* Photographs by Paul Conklin. New York: Putnam, 1989. An intimate look at small-town ranch and farm life in a rural New Mexico community is presented through interviews with local residents and expressive photographs. The rigors of daily life are described along with its festive moments.

Bartone, Elisa. *American Too.* Illustrated by Ted Lewin. New York: Lothrop, Lee & Shepard, 1996. Based on a true story, this book tells how Rosina, recently arrived in New York from Italy after World War I, finds her own way of becoming an American. Lewin's beautiful illustrations convey emotion and complement the text.

Beattie, Owen, and John Geiger with Shelley Tanaka. *Buried in Ice.* New York: Scholastic, 1992. A rousing adventure of searching for two ships that were lost trying to sail the Northwest Passage in 1845. Beattie, an anthropologist, shows how scientists unravel clues and evaluate evidence.

Beirne, Barbara. *Siobhan's Journey: A Belfast Girl Visits the United States.* Minneapolis, MN: Carolrhoda Books, 1993. Ten-year-old Siobhan's first-person narrative tells of her 6-week visit to New Jersey sponsored by Project Children. She compares the peaceful everyday life here, the picnics, and friendly community celebrations with her life in strife-torn Northern Ireland in terms children can readily understand. The photographs make it all come alive.

Bial, Raymond. *Frontier Home*. Boston: Houghton Mifflin, 1993. The pioneer life of the early 1800s is described with emphasis on the building of log cabins, their furnishings, and how these dwellings became frontier homes. Challenges of daily life are also discussed. Color photographs support the text.

Biesty, Stephen. *Cross-Sections: Castle*. London: Dorling Kindersley, 1994. Intricately detailed illustrations reveal the construction of a medieval castle and the daily life within its walls. A glossary defines the specialized vocabulary.

Bowen, Betsy. *Gathering: A Northwoods Counting Book*. Boston: Little, Brown, 1995. Using a counting format from 0 to 12 and illustrated with colorful woodcuts, the author describes life in Minnesota. Each season of the year is presented.

Brandenburg, Jim. *To the Top of the World: Adventures with Arctic Wolves*. New York: Walker, 1993. Dramatic, up-close photos document the adventures of 5-week-old wolf cubs during the Arctic summer. Readers follow the cubs' first forays outside their den in this photo essay showing wolves as nonthreatening creatures in their natural habitat.

Brandenburg, Jim. *Sand and Fog: Adventures in South Africa*. New York: Walker, 1994. A National Geographic photographer, the author presents stunning photographs of animals in their natural habitats, from waterhole to desert to natural game preserve, and of the people who live among them. The text focuses on the people and their unique culture.

Brisson, Pat. *Kate Heads West*. Illustrated by Rick Brown. New York: Bradbury, 1990. Letters are used to describe the natural landscape, history, and cultural sites of four southwestern states. As Kate travels with her friend's family, she writes to her family back home; the cartoon-like illustrations present pictures of state flowers and local vegetation to complement the text.

Brooks, Bruce. *Making Sense: Animal Perception and Communication*. New York: Farrar Straus Giroux, 1993. A visually stunning exploration of the five familiar senses, plus the sense of vibration and movement, which allows animals to perceive potential danger and react in time. Encourages inquiry, class discussion, hypothesis formulation, and further research.

Brown, Mary Barrett. *Wings Along the Waterway*. New York: Orchard, 1992. An oversize book with beautiful paintings describing twenty different birds that live on or near the water. The brief accompanying text describes the birds' physical characteristics and tells how each one interacts with its environment.

Burleigh, Robert. *Flight: The Journey of Charles Lindbergh*. Illustrated by Mike Wimmer. New York: Philomel, 1991. Dramatic double-spread paintings portray Lindbergh's solo flight across the Atlantic in 1927. The exciting text draws readers into Lindbergh's flight activities, braving fog and rain with no radio and landing in Paris 33 1/2 exciting hours after departing New York.

Chang, Ina. *A Separate Battle: Women and the Civil War.* New York: Lodestar, 1991. Women of every color and political stripe participated in the Civil War in every capacity, even as spies and soldiers. Included with the text are historical anecdotes, excerpts from journals, quotations, and other first-person sources that lend an air of freshness and immediacy to the material.

Cherry, Lynne. *A River Ran Wild: An Environmental History.* San Diego, CA: Harcourt Brace, 1992. Traces the history of the Nashua River from its earliest settlement by Native Americans, through logging activities of early settlers, to its pollution in the industrial age. Text and illustrations emphasize efforts of ordinary citizens to stop pollution and restore the river to its former glory.

Cobb, Vicki, and Josh Cobb. *Light Action: Amazing Experiments with Optics.* New York: HarperCollins, 1993. Readers have an opportunity to learn the properties of light through hands-on experience. Prisms, lenses, shadows, colors, and reflections are among some of the topics covered; interesting and meaningful activities are suggested and ample illustrations and diagrams are provided.

Cobb, Vicki, and Kathy Darling. *Wanna Bet? Science Challenges to Fool You.* Illustrated by Meredith Johnson. New York: Lothrop, Lee & Shepard, 1993. This book of "magic" science tricks, based on sound scientific principles, will delight budding scientists. The "tricks" and how to perform them are explained in careful detail that children can readily understand.

Cohen, Barbara. *Molly's Pilgrim.* Illustrated by Michael Deraney. New York: Lothrop, Lee & Shepard, 1983. When Molly, a recent Russian immigrant, is teased by her third-grade classmates about her accent and foreign ways, she is devastated. Her mother and teacher help her understand the true meaning of America as a welcome haven for all "pilgrims."

Cole, Joanna. *The Magic School Bus in the Time of the Dinosaurs.* Illustrated by Bruce Degen. New York: Scholastic, 1994. Combining humor and scientific information, Ms. Frizzle takes her class on a magic bus trip back to the Mesozoic era. They observe and write reports about the plants and dinosaurs, observe fossilized teeth, make a video, and learn how a dinosaur dig is conducted.

Cole, Joanna. *The Magic School Bus Inside a Hurricane.* Illustrated by Bruce Degen. New York: Scholastic, 1995. The magic school bus is transformed into a hot air balloon to take Ms. Frizzle and her class inside a hurricane. Information is conveyed through the text, dialog, illustrations, and short reports by the children.

Cone, Molly. *Come Back, Salmon: How a Group of Dedicated Kids Adopted Pigeon Creek and Brought It Back to Life.* Photographs by Sidnee Wheelwright. San Francisco: Sierra Club Books, 1992. A fine example of presenting children with a problem and having them help organize and execute the solution. It works as a social studies and science book, and the sharp photos emphasize the children's participation.

Conrad, Pam. *Prairie Songs.* Illustrated by Darryl Zudeck. New York: HarperCollins, 1985. Recreates the loneliness and uncertainties faced by settlers on the Nebraska prairie in the last century. Through the first-person narrative of Louisa, a young girl, readers are given a realistic portrait of the indomitable pioneer determination to survive.

Conrad, Pam. *Prairie Visions: The Life and Times of Solomon Butcher.* Photographs by Solomon Butcher. New York: HarperCollins, 1991. Using Butcher's own photographs taken at the end of the last century, Conrad immortalizes early settlers of the Nebraska prairie. Butcher captured the stark reality of the time and place and the settlers' courageous will to succeed in this photodocumentary book.

Cooper, Michael L. *Playing America's Game: The Story of Negro League Baseball.* New York: Lodestar/Dutton, 1993. The Negro Leagues flourished in the 1930s and 1940s, and this profusely illustrated volume captures the camaraderie as well as demeaning hardships faced by the black teams as they barnstormed the country in the years before professional baseball was integrated by Jackie Robinson in 1947.

Cummings, Pat (Ed.). *Talking with Artists.* New York: Bradbury, 1992. Fourteen noted children's book illustrators answer a series of questions typically asked by their child readers and supply biographical information about how they became artists. Full-color examples representative of their artwork complete the biographical sketches and convey the artists' enthusiasm for their work.

Davis, Ossie. *Escape to Freedom: A Play about Young Frederick Douglass.* New York: Viking, 1978. Events from the early life of Frederick Douglass are dramatically portrayed, leaving students to interpret how those events shaped his adult life. The staging can be as simple or elaborate as the class can manage, and the cast of seven characters can be expanded to include the entire class.

Dixon, Dougal. *Dougal Dixon's Dinosaurs.* Honesdale, PA: Boyds Mills Press, 1993. This works as a reference book yet is exciting enough to read from cover to cover. It shows how scientists theorize, form hypotheses, and then attempt to confirm them. Vibrant illustrations show what dinosaurs may have looked like and comparisons with modern-day animals. Bears the Dinosaur Society stamp of recommendation.

Dorris, Michael. *Morning Girl.* New York: Hyperion, 1992. It is 1492 and Morning Girl and her brother Star Boy enjoy a peaceful life on their Caribbean island until Morning Girl discovers the arrival of a shipful of strange-looking men. This historical novel ends with Columbus's arrival and includes an authentic and upsetting excerpt from his log.

Dunphy, Madeleine. *Here Is the Arctic Winter.* Illustrated by Alan Robinson. New York: Hyperion, 1993. Using the familiar format of a cumulative children's rhyme, the diversity and vitality of Arctic life and landscape are described. The illustrations capture the sense of the snowbound scene.

Ekoomiak, Normee. *Arctic Memories.* New York: Holt, 1988. Using a bilingual Inuit and English text, the author/artist recalls his now vanished boyhood in the Canadian arctic. His acrylic paintings poignantly reveal an era when Inuit values and traditions were unquestioned.

Filipovic, Zlata. *Zlata's Diary: A Child's Life in Sarajevo.* New York: Viking, 1994. The ravages of the war in Sarajevo and its consequent effects on the teen-age author are described in graphic detail. Readers feel the bombs exploding all around them and stomachs rumbling with hunger in this vivid, first-person account by a sensitive observer.

Fisher, Leonard Everett. *Ellis Island: Gateway to the New World.* New York: Holiday House, 1986. While giving the history of Ellis Island as the entry point for millions of immigrants in the early years of this century, Fisher raises the issue of how U.S. immigration policy is decided. Archival photographs are used, as are original drawings and maps by the author.

Fisher, Leonard Everett. *The Great Wall of China.* New York: Macmillan, 1986. Acrylic paintings in shades of black and gray help trace the story of China's Great Wall, begun about 2,200 years ago to protect the Chinese from Mongol invaders. Chinese characters describing the illustrations appear on each page, with their English translation provided at the end of the book.

Fleischman, Paul. *Bull Run.* Illustrated by David Frampton. New York: HarperCollins, 1993. Through the first-person voices of sixteen characters, readers live through the opening salvos of the Civil War. Northerners and Southerners tell their stories, sparing no details. Some of the characters are real; all the events actually occurred.

Fleischman, Paul. *Copier Creations.* Illustrated by David Cain. New York: HarperCollins, 1993. Gives directions for using copy machines to create stationery, films, stencils, flip books, and much more. The directions are easy to follow, and accompanying illustrations are clear and simple.

Flint, Russ. *Let's Build a House: A White Cottage Before Winter.* Nashville, TN: Ideals Children's Books, 1990. Through text and watercolor illustrations, children follow the process of one family building a house. Written in the first person by a fictional girl, Dorinda, this picture book introduces young children to types of tasks and people involved in house construction.

Freedman, Florence B. *Two Tickets to Freedom: The True Story of Ellen and William Craft, Fugitive Slaves.* Illustrated by Ezra Jack Keats. New York: Simon and Schuster, 1971. Based on authentic primary-source material, this book traces the escape of a slave couple from Macon, Georgia to Canada and eventually to England. Details of their difficult and dangerous journey convey the hazards frequently encountered by escaping slaves.

Freedman, Russell. *Immigrant Kids.* New York: Dutton, 1980. In what would become his singular trademark, Freedman uses archival photographs to enhance his meticulous research. Here in a highly readable format he writes about the lives of young immigrants before there were laws protecting them from exploitation in the labor force or health and education codes to ensure healthy childhoods.

Freedman, Russell. *Lincoln, a Photobiography.* New York: Clarion, 1987. Pioneering the photobiography form for which he is justly known, Freedman provides a picture of a real human being, not an untarnished icon. From Lincoln's boyhood to his years in the White House, Freedman's meticulous research gives readers a sense of a real person, a father, and a president.

Freedman, Russell. *The Wright Brothers: How They Invented the Airplane.* New York: Clarion, 1991. Freedman writes about the contributions of Orville and Wilbur Wright to developing a workable flying machine. He includes information about the efforts of others important to flight's early history. Most interesting, he uses the Wrights' own photographs that document their first efforts.

Freedman, Russell. *Eleanor: A Life of Discovery.* New York: Clarion, 1993. Another photobiography uses historic photos and personal anecdotes that reflect the author's solid research. Readers are treated to a dynamic portrait of a First Lady who spoke her mind and championed causes that benefited humanity at a time when women were rarely seen in public or were so unabashedly outspoken.

Fritz, Jean. *Harriet Beecher Stowe and the Beecher Preachers.* New York: Putnam, 1994. The life of the author who wrote *Uncle Tom's Cabin* is chronicled in this fascinating and well-researched biography. Illustrated with photographs, the book includes a Beecher Stowe family tree, author's notes, and an index.

Fritz, Jean. *You Want Women to Vote, Lizzie Stanton?* Illustrated by DyAnne DiSalvo-Ryan. New York: Putnam, 1995. With humor and insight, Jean Fritz has written this biography of Elizabeth Cady

Stanton, one of America's most noted women suffragettes. Includes author's notes, a bibliography, and index.

Gardner, Robert, and Dennis Shortelle. *The Forgotten Players: The Story of Black Baseball in America*. New York: Walker, 1993. In true sports books fashion, this volume recounts the usual statistics. What makes it memorable is its social history. Through the accomplishments of African American players a social history of racial prejudice and social injustice is dramatically portrayed. Readers live the hostility, grueling barnstorming schedule, and humiliation of having to sleep on the bus back when black teams were not allowed to check into hotels.

George, Jean Craighead. *The First Thanksgiving*. Illustrated by Thomas Locker. New York: Philomel, 1993. A compelling narrative with powerful illustrations that boldly reinforce the Pilgrims' dramatic adventure. The contributions of Squanto and the Pawtuxet tribe, without whom the Pilgrims would not have survived the harsh New England winter and celebrated the first Harvest Feast, are sensitively portrayed.

George, Jean Craighead. *The Wild, Wild Cookbook: A Guide for Young Wild-Food Foragers*. Illustrated by Walter Kessell. New York: Crowell, 1982. Divided into seasonal sections, this book contains information on identifying, gathering, and cooking wild plants. Recipes for plants such as dandelions, acorns, and pinyon pine are included. Kessell's line drawings support the text.

Gibbons, Gail. *Spiders*. New York: Holiday House, 1993. Gibbons's characteristic graphic artwork in poster-bright colors provides an excellent backdrop for this introduction to spiders. The clear, simple text explains the difference between spiders and insects, and provides details about several varieties of spiders.

Gibbons, Gail. *Nature's Green Umbrella: Tropical Rain Forests*. New York: Morrow, 1994. Vivid watercolors that are the author/illustrator's trademark introduce readers to plant and animal life of the tropical rain forest. The simply worded text, appearing in margin sidebars, introduces scientific terms, ecological concepts, and ways to protect endangered rain forests.

Gibbons, Gail. *The Reasons for Seasons*. New York: Holiday House, 1995. This colorful picture book explains how the Earth's changing relation to the sun causes the various seasons. Several pages of text and illustrations describe each season in language appropriate for primary-age children.

Giblin, James Cross. *Let There Be Light: A Book about Windows*. New York: Crowell, 1988. Windows come in different shapes and for different reasons. Giblin explores their design and purpose throughout history and in different locations. Photographs and prints support the text.

Giblin, James Cross. *The Riddle of the Rosetta Stone: Key to Ancient Egypt.* New York: Crowell, 1990. Writing like a mystery novelist, Giblin tracks down clues scientists followed that finally revealed the key to the Rosetta stone's hieroglyphic symbols, enabling them to unlock secrets of ancient Egyptian history and culture.

Giblin, James Cross. *The Skyscraper Book.* Illustrated by Anthony Kramer; photographs by David Anderson. New York: HarperCollins, 1981. Besides giving a comprehensive history of American skyscrapers, Giblin provides details on the construction of different styles of skyscrapers. He explains why different construction methods and materials are used, giving mathematical information on construction and site plans and the geometric rationale for the various constructions.

Gold, Carol. *Science Express: 50 Scientific Stunts from the Ontario Science Centre.* Illustrated by Vesna Krstanovich. Reading, MA: Addison-Wesley, 1991. Thirty-six experiments, all scientifically accurate, will convince children that science is fun and has real-life application. Cartoon illustrations further enhance this light-hearted approach to science.

Goldish, Meish. *Immigration: How Should It Be Controlled?* New York: 21st Century Books, 1994. The question of whether it is a good policy to keep the doors open for immigrants to enter the United States is presented in terms young readers can readily understand. Current citizenship requirements and laws are discussed. A historical perspective on immigration is provided through the text, color-coded charts, and graphs.

Granfield, Linda. *Extra! Extra!: The Who, What, Where, When, and Why of Newspapers.* Illustrated by Bill Slavin. New York: Orchard, 1994. "How to" put together a newspaper including news stories, feature stories, editorials, and comics. Interesting, fun projects help children learn how to do it themselves. Anecdotes from journalists and sprightly illustrations enliven the text.

Greenfield, Howard. *The Hidden Children.* New York: Ticknor & Fields, 1993. Thirteen Holocaust survivors recount the anguish of being separated from their families, of having to keep silent, and the constant fear of being discovered. First-person narratives and use of original photos create a dramatic emotional effect.

Greenlaw, Jean M. *Ranch Dressing: The Story of Western Wear.* New York: Dutton/Lodestar, 1993. A very readable discussion of how western attire such as boots and ten-gallon hats evolved in response to cowboys' needs while riding the range, herding bulls, enduring dramatic weather changes, and mending fences.

Hall, Katy, and Lisa Eisenberg. *Batty Riddles.* Illustrated by Nicole Rubel. New York: Dial, 1993. Slapstick illustrations accompany silly riddles and rhymes about bats. Some are based on readers' knowledge of bat facts, and all explore aspects of English language usage.

Hamilton, Virginia. *Many Thousands Gone: African Americans from Slavery to Freedom.* Illustrated by Leo and Diane Dillon. New York: Knopf, 1993. Traces the history of slavery in America from its beginning through its final days. Personal portraits depict the hardships, indignities, and efforts at escape along the underground railroad. Emotionally charged illustrations mirror the harsh effect of the eloquent text.

Hansen-Smith, Bradford. *The Hands-On Marvelous Ball Book.* New York: Scientific American, 1995. Geometric concepts are introduced in rhymed text and humorous illustrations. With three household items—paper plates, tape, and bobby pins—children can follow directions to make a ball, tetrahedron, octahedron, and torus ring.

Harrison, Ted. *O Canada.* New York: Ticknor & Fields, 1993. With the words of the Canadian national anthem as the book's basic text, the history, geography, and important information about each province are given. Boldly colored, double-page illustrations portray Canada's rugged beauty.

Haskins, James. *The March on Washington.* New York: HarperCollins, 1993. The 1963 civil rights March on Washington with all of its tensions and drama is chronicled. Notes about behind-the-scenes planning among leaders of the march and an introduction by James Farmer impart a tone of excitement to the text.

Haskins, Jim. *Count Your Way Through Korea.* Illustrated by Dennis Hockerman. Minneapolis, MN: Carolrhoda Books, 1989. In a brief introduction for young readers, using the numbers 1 through 10, the culture, traditions, and customs of Korea are explored. The illustrations capture the flavor and essence of old Korea and its position as a modern industrial nation.

Haskins, Jim. *Count Your Way Through India.* Illustrated by Liz Brenner Dodson. Minneapolis, MN: Carolrhoda Books, 1989. Another title in the "Count Your Way..." series, this uses the same double-page format for the numbers 1 to 10. The meaning of any foreign terms used in the text is made clear, and a guide to phonetic pronunciation is provided. The illustrations clarify the text for readers.

Haskins, Jim. *Get on Board: The Story of the Underground Railroad.* New York: Scholastic, 1993. The unique organization of this book highlights stories of individuals who helped slaves escape. There is a section about "conductors," another about "train robbers" (those who captured and returned escaping slaves).

Hausman, Gerald. *Turtle Island ABC: A Gathering of Native American Symbols.* Illustrated by Cara and Barry Moser. New York:

HarperCollins, 1994. This alphabet book features signs and symbols significant to Native American tribal life. Each object or symbol is identified by name and its significance is explained in lyric prose. The Mosers' illustrations represent the palette associated with Native American life, especially in the Southwest.

Hendrich, Paula. *Saving America's Birds.* New York: Lothrop, Lee & Shepard, 1982. Recounts efforts to save various species of American birds that have been declared endangered. When used with more recently published titles, it can help children determine the success or failure of early attempts to reduce ecological devastation and rescue endangered species of birds.

Hoobler, Dorothy, and Thomas Hoobler. *The Italian American Family Album.* New York: Oxford, 1994. This uses primary-source material such as excerpts from diaries, letters, and recorded histories to document the immigrant experience. Memories of their first days here, finding jobs, reuniting with relatives, and of nostalgia for the old country are universal to all immigrant groups.

Hopkinson, Deborah. *Sweet Clara and the Freedom Quilt.* Illustrated by James Ransome. New York: Knopf, 1993. Sweet Clara, a young slave working in the Big House, learns to sew and stitches a quilt that serves as a map for slaves seeking freedom along the Underground Railroad. Clara and Young Jack eventually use the quilt themselves to escape to freedom.

Hoyt-Goldsmith, Diane. *Arctic Hunter.* Photographs by Lawrence Migdale. New York: Holiday House, 1992. This photo essay tells about everyday events in the life of a 10-year-old Inupiat boy living north of the Arctic Circle in Alaska. It presents the contrasts, as well as the conflicts, between traditional Inupiat ways and the encroachment of contemporary society and technology.

Hoyt-Goldsmith, Diane. *Celebrating Kwanzaa.* Photographs by Lawrence Migdale. New York: Holiday House, 1993. A first-person narrative in the voice of a 10-year-old child recalls a warm family celebration of the African-American holiday, Kwanzaa. The text explains aspects of the celebration and the meaning of its symbols. Appealing full-color photos highlight family members celebrating this festive holiday.

Hulme, Joy N. *Sea Sums.* Illustrated by Carol Schwartz. New York: Hyperion, 1996. Rhymed text presents addition and subtraction problems related to sea life. Colorful paintings that cover the entire page illustrate the problems. Explanatory information at the end of the book gives more details about the sea creatures found in the text.

Hunt, Jonathan. *Illuminations.* New York: Bradbury, 1989. Using the art of an illustrated manuscript, this medieval-style alphabet book explains objects used in the Middle Ages and names from Arthurian legend. Sidebars running down and across the pages offer further explanations of the objects' social significance.

Isaacson, Philip M. *Round Buildings, Square Buildings, and Buildings That Wiggle Like a Fish.* New York: Knopf, 1988. Clear, crisp color photographs taken by the author show architectural styles around the world. Chapters focus on such topics as light and color, pathways, doorways, ornaments, and indoor skies. More information about the structures featured in the book is provided at the end.

Jacobs, Francine. *The Tainos: The People Who Welcomed Columbus.* Illustrated by Patrick Collins. New York: Putnam, 1992. After providing readers with the history and culture of the Tainos living on Hispaniola when Columbus arrived in 1492, Jacobs describes their destruction in detail. While emphasizing the Tainos's agricultural way of life, the book details how they were enslaved at first and then succumbed to diseases brought by Europeans to their island home.

James, Simon. *Dear Mr. Blueberry.* New York: Macmillan, 1991. Through a series of letters written to her teacher, Mr. Blueberry, Emily learns all about the whale she insists lives in her backyard pond. The situation's humor is portrayed through cartoon drawings.

Jaspersohn, William. *Cookies.* New York: Macmillan, 1993. This photo essay explains how one of children's favorite snacks is made. It takes readers from the initial milling of the flour and manufacture of chocolate chips through preparation of the dough, baking, and commercial distribution.

Johnson, Steven T. *Alphabet City.* NY: Viking/Penguin; 1995. A visually stunning tour of New York City architectural sites inviting readers to discover the alphabet in familiar constructions such as the towers of the Brooklyn Bridge, a fire escape, and the window of a Gothic church. Invites children to walk through their neighborhood taking a fresh look at familiar objects. A Caledcott Honor book.

Kendall, Russ. *Eskimo Boy: Life in an Inupiaq Eskimo Village.* New York: Scholastic, 1992. Presents the daily routines of a young boy living on an island off the northwest coast of Alaska in an outstanding color photo essay. Good supporting materials for multicultural units and social studies.

Knight, Amelia Stewart. *The Way West: Journal of a Pioneer Woman.* Illustrated by Michael McCurdy. New York: Simon and Schuster, 1993. A beautiful adaptation of the 1853 diary of Amelia Stewart Knight, which she scribed as she and her family traveled west by wagon from Iowa to the Oregon Territory. Powerful illustrations pull readers into the journey's difficulties and triumphs. Useful in pioneer studies as well as to encourage children's journal writings.

Krull, Kathleen. *Lives of Musicians: Good Times, Bad Times ... and What the Neighbors Thought.* Illustrated by Kathryn Hewitt. San Diego,

CA: Harcourt Brace, 1993. Twenty European and American composers are introduced in brief entries, with witty, humorous style. In addition to well-known facts, the sections also contain some little-known information that enlivens the musicians' histories.

Lacey, Elizabeth A. *What's the Difference? A Guide to Some Familiar Animal Look-Alikes.* Illustrated by Robert Shetterly. New York: Clarion, 1993. Seven essays, illustrated with informative pen-and-ink drawings, clearly describe the similarities and differences in physical characteristics and behavior of pairs of animals that are similar in appearance, such as tortoise and turtle, alligator and crocodile, bison and buffalo. Short text offers challenging, enjoyable reading for children who have serious interest in animals.

Lankford, Mary D. *Hopscotch Around the World.* Illustrated by Karen Milone. New York: Morrow, 1992. Hopscotch, a universal game of childhood, is celebrated in this collection of nineteen hopscotch games from all over the world. Rules and patterns are clearly given so readers can try any version of the game themselves. Primary- and middle-graders will enjoy reading and playing with the book.

Lasky, Kathryn. *Dinosaur Dig.* Photographs by Christopher Knight. New York: Morrow, 1990. Accounts of a family's trip to Montana's Badlands to hunt for fossils along with five other families. Children and adults get down on their knees to sniff dirt, crawl along cliffs, search for bones, seal them with resin, and make plaster casts.

Lasky, Kathryn. *Surtsey: The Newest Place on Earth.* Photographs by Christopher Knight. New York: Hyperion, 1992. Describes in detail the formation, naming, and colonization of the 33-year-old volcanic island Surtsey—the newest land on earth. Information is also provided on how the first plants and animals became established there. The quotations that open each chapter, adapted from an Icelandic epic, poetically weave the book together.

Lauber, Patricia. *The News about Dinosaurs.* New York: Bradbury, 1989. Updates information and clarifies misconceptions about dinosaurs. Entries include the discovery of four new dinosaurs, the different gaits dinosaurs had, the fact that dinosaurs lived in herds, and the ways dinosaurs cared for their young. The text is rendered in attractive, accessible design, with large, vivid, striking illustrations.

Leedy, Loreen. *The Furry News: How to Make a Newspaper.* New York: Holiday House, 1990. A group of imaginative animals collect, write, and print the news in a cartoon format while readers learn the basic procedures of making a neighborhood newspaper. Ideal for primary-graders for learning writing and reporting skills.

Leedy, Loreen. *Messages in the Mailbox: How to Write a Letter.* New York: Holiday House, 1991. In this inviting how-to book with accessible, cartoon-like illustrations, an alligator teacher takes her class through the art of personal letters, business letters, letters for complaint, and more. Useful in creative writing classes for primary grades.

Leedy, Loreen. *Postcards from Pluto: A Tour of the Solar System.* New York: Holiday House, 1993. A group of young astronauts and their robot guide explore the solar system. The space travelers send back to Earth postcards full of intriguing facts and information they discover en route. The particular postcard format is engaging and can be easily adapted to other themes in science projects or creative writing classes.

Leigh, Nila K. *Learning to Swim in Swaziland: A Child's-Eye View of a Southern African Country.* New York: Scholastic, 1993. Depicts the life in Swaziland from a young American girl's perspective. Text is in a child's handwriting, and original illustrations include drawings, photos, and other travel items such as currency, stamps, and passport.

Lessem, Don. *Dinosaur Worlds: New Dinosaurs, New Discoveries.* Honesdale, PA: Boyds Mills Press, 1996. Illustrated with full-color pictures and photographs, this book presents the most recent discoveries about dinosaurs. Did you know that Tyrannosaurus Rex is no longer the largest meat-eating dinosaur—Gigantosaurus is? This is one of the many new discoveries that are revealed in the book. A glossary and index are included.

Lester, Julius. *To Be a Slave.* Illustrated by Tom Feelings. New York: Dial, 1968. First-hand accounts of the auction block, plantation life, resistance to slavery, emancipation, and post-emancipation times are excerpted from nineteenth-century slave narratives. The quotations, accompanied by somber black-and-white pictures, are arranged in chronological order. Valuable material for in-depth understanding of slavery in American history.

Levine, Ellen. *Freedom's Children: Young Civil Rights Activists Tell Their Own Stories.* New York: Putnam, 1993. Thirty African American people who were children and teenagers at the time of the civil rights movement tell their experience in their own words. Collectively it is the story of a political and social movement that changed America. Background information is added to each chapter, and striking black-and-white photos bring readers into the historical moments.

Lewington, Anna. *Antonio's Rain Forest.* Photographs by Edward Parker. Minneapolis, MN: Carolrhoda Books, 1993. Antonio lives in the Amazon rain forest in Brazil and describes his daily life and how his community makes rubber from the rubber trees. Color photographs with captions containing information complement the text. A glossary, things readers can do to help save the rain forest, and an index are included.

Love, Ann, and Jane Drake. *Take Action: An Environmental Book for Kids.* New York: Morrow, 1992. Discusses the importance of nature and healthy environment, the endangered animals and plants, and what young people can do to protect the earth and living things. Full of useful information, engaging illustrations, and guidance for actions and projects, the volume is valuable for both home readings and school projects.

Lyons, Mary E. *Letters from a Slave Girl: The Story of Harriet Jacobs.* New York: Scribner's, 1992. Based on Harriet Jacob's own 1861 autobiography, the book reveals in vivid detail what thousands of African American women endured in the dark era of American history. The first part is composed of fictionalized letters that centered around the first half of Jacobs's life; her later years are briefly recounted in the second section.

Macaulay, David. *Castle.* New York: Houghton Mifflin, 1977. This Caldecott Honor Book describes the planning and construction of a fictional castle in Wales in the thirteenth century. Macaulay's intricate pen-and-ink drawings, which include the castle's floor plan, enhance the text.

Macaulay, David. *Pyramid.* New York: Houghton Mifflin, 1975. The laborious, careful process of building an Egyptian pyramid is described through text and pen-and-ink illustrations. Each step is explained and illustrated. A glossary is provided.

MacGregor, Carol. *The Fairy Tale Cookbook.* Pictures by Debby L. Carter. New York: Macmillan, 1982. A collection of twenty-five recipes for a variety of dishes inspired by famous tales such as "Snow White," "Puss in Boots," "Stone Soup," and "Hansel and Gretel." Each recipe is introduced by a brief summary and direct quotation from the original tale. Valuable resource for young children who are enthusiastic to bring their favorite tales to life (and to the table).

Macy, Sue. *A Whole New Ball Game: The Story of the All-American Girls Professional Baseball League.* New York: Holt, 1993. Describes the history, development, and activities of the members of the All-American Girls Professional Baseball League, the women's professional baseball league that existed between 1943 and 1954. Balancing voices of the league's women with a lively, insightful overview of the changing patterns of American life, the book will attract children who are serious sports fans or interested in American history and women's movements.

Martin, James. *Hiding Out: Camouflage in the Wild.* Photographs by Art Wolfe. New York: Crown, 1993. Close-up color photographs of animals help readers understand the concept of camouflage and how animals use it to survive. Natural selection is also explained.

Matthews, Downs. *Arctic Summer.* Photographs by Dan Guravich. New York: Simon and Schuster, 1993. Arctic animals, plants, and lands are elegantly presented in excellent photographs with brief explanations. The smoothly blended introduction to the Arctic world adds up to an appealing, informative volume.

Matthews, Downs. *Polar Bear Cubs.* Photographs by Dan Guravich. New York: Simon and Schuster, 1989. This photo essay follows the polar bear family—a mother bear and her two cubs—through the cubs' first year of life in their Arctic habitat. The simple, easy-to-read text also introduces other animals living in the same region. The excellent photos are especially appealing. A good introduction for young readers.

McKissack, Patricia C., and Fredrick McKissack, Jr. *Black Diamond: The Story of the Negro Baseball Leagues.* New York: Scholastic, 1994. Describes historical accounts of the great African-American baseball players, such as Cool Papa Bell, Satchel Paige, and Bee Ball, who formed their own Negro Leagues when segregation shut them out of major league baseball. Useful as an integral part of sports history for multicultural studies.

McKissack, Patricia C., and Fredrick L. McKissack. *Christmas in the Big House, Christmas in the Quarters.* Illustrated by John Thompson. New York: Scholastic, 1994. Vividly describes events of the 1859 Christmas season in a Virginia plantation and its slave quarters. Text in parallel tracks compares and contrasts celebrations and activities in the different settings; realistic illustrations provide insight and detail of the time.

McMahon, Patricia. *Chi-hoon: A Korean Girl.* Photographs by Michael O'Brien. Honesdale, PA: Boyds Mills Press, 1993. Presents a week in the life of an 8-year-old, middle-class Korean girl in a day-by-day diary format. High-quality photographs and comprehensive pronunciation guide contribute to the book's accessibility. Informative source of contemporary Korean society in social studies.

Meltzer, Milton. *The Amazing Potato.* New York: HarperCollins, 1992. A salute to the plain daily subject; a comprehensive, highly readable introduction to the history, events, types, and current uses of potatoes in the world marketplace. As the subtitle suggests, "A story in which the Incas, Conquistadors, Marie Antoinette, Thomas Jefferson, wars, famines, immigrants, and French fries all play a part."

Meltzer, Milton. *Lincoln: In His Own Words.* San Diego, CA: Harcourt, Brace, 1993. Insightful text combines background commentary with quotes from Lincoln's letters, speeches, and public papers. Valuable reference in history units and good material for read-aloud.

Melville, Herman. *Catskill Eagle.* Paintings by Thomas Locker. New York: Philomel, 1991. Inspired by words depicting the eagle of the Catskill Mountains in Melville's classic novel Moby Dick, the artist's breathtaking paintings reconstruct the world of the mighty bird in nature.

Mettger, Zak. *Till Victory Is Won: Black Soldiers in the Civil War.* New York: Lodestar, 1994. Based on first-person accounts, historical documents, and illustrated with archival photographs and fine drawings, this volume tells the little-known story of how black Americans gained the right to fight in the Civil War and went on to make distinguished contributions on and off the battlefield.

Miller, Margaret. *Can You Guess?* New York: Greenwillow, 1993. Suggests both right and wrong answers to daily-life questions of youngsters such as "What do you comb in the morning?" "What do you plant in the ground?" with excellent pictures of children of various ethnic groups. Superb for stimulating interactive play and logical thinking of preschool and kindergarten children.

Morley, Jacqueline. *An Egyptian Pyramid.* Illustrated by Mark Bergin and John James. New York: Peter Bedrick Books, 1991. Text and illustrations work seamlessly together to describe the construction of an Egyptian pyramid, mummification, and the city of the dead. A glossary and index are included. Rosalie David, a British Egyptologist, served as consultant for the book.

Morris, Desmond. *The World of Animals.* New York: Viking, 1993. Armed with careful research, detailed illustrations, and anecdotal stories, the respected naturalist tells stories of familiar and famous wild animals, many of them endangered. The carefully written entries record the special way in which each animal lives, mates, rears the young, and survives in today's world.

Murphy, Jim. *The Boys' War: Confederate and Union Soldiers Talk about the Civil War.* Boston: Houghton Mifflin, 1990. Basing his writing on careful research including letters and diaries, Murphy examines the participation of boys younger than 16 who were soldiers in the Civil War. Photographs bring these boys and their experiences to life in this well-written and insightful book.

Murphy, Jim. *The Long Road to Gettysburg.* New York: Clarion, 1992. Depicts the actual events of the Civil War Battle of Gettysburg in 1863 as seen through the eyes of two participants of opposite camps—a Confederate lieutenant and a Union soldier. Carefully organized and written text is illustrated by drawings and archival photographs and concludes with an endnote recording the life of two men after the war.

Murphy, Jim. *Across America on an Emigrant Train.* New York: Clarion, 1993. Due to his limited budget, Robert Louis Stevenson traveled across the American continent on an emigrant train and experienced the discomforts endured by the immigrants. The memoir is supplemented with historical details about the construction of the railroad lines, the railroad workers, and the displacement of Native Americans.

Murphy, Stuart J. *Give Me Half! Understanding Halves.* Illustrated by G. Brian Karras. New York: HarperCollins, 1996. A title in the "MathStart" series for primary-grade children, this book presents fractions as part of our everyday life. Humor is conveyed in the text and colorful illustrations.

Murphy, Stuart J. *A Pair of Socks.* Illustrated by Lois Ehlert. New York: HarperCollins, 1996. Appropriate for preschool and primary-grade children, this book presents the concept of matching through the perspective of a striped sock looking for its missing mate. Full-color illustrations by an award-winning artist reinforce the concept.

Murphy, Stuart J. *Get Up and Go!* Illustrated by Diane Greenseid. New York: HarperCollins, 1996. Rhymed text explains the concept of time lines and addition to young children. Color illustrations of a young girl getting ready for school with help from her dog support the development of the concept.

Musgrove, Margaret. *Ashanti to Zulu: African Traditions.* Illustrated by Leo and Diane Dillon. New York: Dial, 1976. Elegant, authentic illustrations amplify brief, alphabetically ordered texts of diverse African tribes and their customs. Offers an insightful glimpse of traditional African lives.

Pandell, Karen. *Land of Dark, Land of Light: The Arctic National Wildlife Refuge.* New York: Dutton, 1993. An outstanding photo essay of the Arctic National Wildlife Refuge, which shelters animals that live and survive on the White Continent. Ideal for reading aloud; also recommended for environmental studies, season change, and Alaskan studies.

Patent, Dorothy Hinshaw. *Where the Bald Eagles Gather.* Photographs by William Muñoz. New York: Clarion, 1984. Gathering annually at Glacier National Park to feast on the spawning kokanee salmon, American bald eagles give natural scientists the opportunity to study their hunting behavior, survival problems, and life cycles. The well-organized text, accompanied with vivid black-and-white photographs, provides a highly informative account of the current state of our national birds.

Patent, Dorothy Hinshaw. *Looking at Penguins.* Photographs by Graham Robertson. New York: Holiday House, 1993. An introductory text of the different species, physical features, hunting and feeding habits, breeding rituals, and the current endangered status of penguins.

Accompanying the informative text, eye-opening, full-color photographs bring these Arctic birds to life.

Penner, Lucille Recht. *Eating the Plates: A Pilgrim Book of Food and Manners.* New York: Macmillan, 1991. A delightful, easy-to-read account of eating habits, customs, and manners of the Pilgrims in New Plymouth colony. Ten representative Pilgrim recipes conclude the book, and the carefully selected illustrations add much flavor to it.

Peterson, Cris. *Extra Cheese, Please: Mozzarella's Journey from Cow to Pizza.* Honesdale, PA: Boyds Mills Press, 1994. An inviting photo essay documents the step-by-step procedure of making mozzarella cheese, from the milk produced on the author's own farm to the cheese factory and finally to home-made pizza. The light, informative text, along with the engaging full-color photos, makes the book highly attractive for primary-graders.

Pinkney, Andrea Davis. *Alvin Ailey.* Illustrated by Brian Pinkney. New York: Hyperion, 1993. Describes the life, dancing, and choreography of Alvin Ailey, who created his own modern dance company to explore and honor the black experience in America. Dynamic scratchboard art highlights the spirit of the renowned African-American modern dance master.

Pinkney, Andrea Davis. *Seven Candles for Kwanzaa.* Illustrated by Brian Pinkney. New York: Dial, 1993. A wonderful introduction to the origins and practices of Kwanzaa, the 7-day festival observed from December 26 through January 1, during which people of African descent celebrate and rejoice in their traditional customs and values. Seven candles are lit during the festival to symbolize Kwanzaa's seven principles.

Pringle, Laurence. *Living in a Risky World.* New York: Morrow, 1989. Thought-provoking discussion of the risks modern society faces every day as people deal with frightening pollution and dangers related to food, clothing, transportation, air, water, disease, natural disasters, and almost every area of human lives. Recommendations for building up a safer and more healthful environment highlight the end of the book.

Pringle, Laurence. *Antarctica: The Last Unspoiled Continent.* New York: Simon and Schuster, 1992. Introduces the geology, climate, history, and human exploration of Antarctica. Updated information, insightful writings, and outstanding pictures build up a highly informative and enjoyable text.

Rappaport, Doreen. *Escape from Slavery: Five Journeys to Freedom.* Illustrated by Charles Lilly. New York: HarperCollins, 1991. Describes in detail the stories of five black slaves who fled to freedom in pre–Civil War days. Fictionalized text is followed by an intensive bibliography and an afterword that discusses relevant resources.

Reynolds, Jan. *Frozen Land: Vanishing Cultures.* San Diego, CA: Harcourt Brace, 1993. Depicts a young girl as she learns the early ways of the Inuit. Stunning photography captures the details of igloo building, fishing, and drum dancing. An authentic, accessible presentation of the traditional life of the North people.

Reynolds, Jan. *Mongolia: Vanishing Cultures*. San Diego, CA: Harcourt Brace, 1994. The author visits a nomadic Mongolian family and records their daily life in a culture facing dramatic changes. Excellent photographs support and extend the text.

Roop, Peter, and Connie Roop. *Off the Map: The Journals of Lewis and Clark*. Illustrated by Tim Tanner. New York: Walker, 1993. Provides brief and readable excerpts from the journal of Lewis and Clark as they met Pres. Jefferson's charge in 1803 to explore the Missouri River, to record the land and its fauna and flora, and to get information about the native population.

Roop, Peter, and Connie Roop. *Stonehenge: Opposing Viewpoints*. San Diego, CA: Greenhaven Press, 1989. The authors pose perplexing questions about Stonehenge, such as who built it and how was it built, and discuss various viewpoints regarding the answers. This book is part of the "Great Mysteries: Opposing Viewpoints" series.

Rosenberg, Maxine B. *Hiding to Survive: Stories of Jewish Children Rescued from the Holocaust*. New York: Clarion, 1994. Biographical accounts of the childhoods of fourteen Jewish children hidden from Nazi persecution during World War II. Individual narratives, told in first person, conclude with postscripts that comment on their feelings five decades later about having been hidden children.

Rounds, Glen. *Sod Houses on the Great Plains*. New York: Holiday House, 1995. Settlers on the Great Plains used prairie sod to build houses. This informational picture book explains, through the author's drawings and text, the construction of sod houses.

Ryden, Hope. *America's Bald Eagle*. New York: Putnam, 1985. Basing the book on two years of observation and study, the author/photographer presents fascinating insights and rare facts about the behavior of America's bald eagle, its population's dramatic decline in many states, and the human efforts now under way to help the symbolic bird make a recovery. A splendidly detailed account of our national bird that will satisfy the interest of middle- and upper-graders.

Sachar, Louis. *Sideways Arithmetic from Wayside School*. New York: Scholastic, 1989. Sideways arithmetic (puzzle-type mathematical problems) is presented in the context of the Wayside School and centers on spelling, lunch, pronouns, et cetera. Hints for solving the problems are provided.

Sattler, Helen Roney. *The Book of Eagles*. Illustrated by Jean Day Zallinger. New York: Lothrop, Lee & Shepard, 1989. Sixty species of eagles from around the world are described in this colorful, oversized volume. The first five chapters discuss physical characteristics, hunting behavior, courting and nesting, care of the young, and the positive and negative impact of human beings; the second half of the book consists of illustrated dictionary entries for all species. Many informative details are included in the illustrations and text, making the volume a first-rate source on this interesting bird family.

Say, Allen. *Grandfather's Journey*. New York: Houghton Mifflin, 1993. In simple, poetic words and quiet, elegant watercolors, the Japanese-American author recounts his grandfather's journey to America and back to Japan, which he later also undertakes, and the feelings of being torn by love for two different countries. An insightful story that will be appreciated by many children in today's multicultural society.

Scieszka, Jon. *Math Curse*. Illustrated by Lane Smith. New York: Viking, 1995. A girl develops math anxiety when her teacher says that "you can think of almost everything as a math problem." Humorous illustrations visually represent the math problems and the girl's "curse."

Scott, Ann Herbert. *Cowboy Country*. Illustrated by Ted Lewin. New York: Clarion, 1993. Written in the first person of an old buckaroo sharing his memories and information about a cowboy's life with a young boy. Lewin's watercolor illustrations vividly portray the Western setting.

Selsam, Millicent, and Joyce Hunt. *A First Look at Owls, Eagles, and Other Hunters of the Sky*. Illustrated by Harriett Springer. New York: Walker, 1986. Presents distinctive physical characteristics of various owl and hawk species, eagles, and vultures. Useful to elementary students as an introduction to birds of prey as well as an exercise in nature observation.

Silver, Donald. *Why Save the Rain Forest?* Illustrated by Patricia J. Wynner. New York: Messner, 1993. The rain forest as home to many living things is described, and reasons for saving it are explained. A map showing rain forests around the world, a list of ways children can help save them, and a list of further readings are included.

Simon, Seymour. *New Questions and Answers about Dinosaurs*. Illustrated by Jennifer Dewey. New York: Morrow, 1990. Twenty-two questions and answers explore the current knowledge about dinosaurs—their size, color, brain, reproduction, and extinction. An updated, concise resource on children's favorite extinct animals.

Simon, Seymour. *Wolves*. New York: HarperCollins, 1993. Stunning color pictures bring readers into an informative photo essay describing and explaining wolf behavior. Discusses this intriguing carnivore's physical characteristics, hunting behaviors, family organization, caring for the young, and human fear about them.

Smithsonian Institution. *Fun Machines: Step-by-Step Science Activity Projects from the Smithsonian Institution.* Milwaukee, WI: Gareth Stevens, 1993. Ten science activities are explained with clear directions for students to follow. The book includes places to write and visit, further reading about fun machines, hands-on facts about fun machines, a glossary, and index.

Sneve, Virginia Driving Hawk. *The Sioux: A First American Book.* Illustrated by Ronald Himler. New York: Holiday House, 1993. Identifies the different tribes of the Sioux and discusses their beliefs and traditional way of life. Aspects of Sioux history and culture are included. Realistic watercolor illustrations enhance the well-organized, informative text.

Stanley, Diane, and Peter Vennema. *Bard of Avon: The Story of William Shakespeare.* Illustrated by Diane Stanley. New York: Morrow, 1992. Biographical information on the British master playwright Shakespeare is woven together with the development of the theater during the era of Queen Elizabeth I and King James I. Stunning double-page illustrations depict typical customs of the time and the interior design of the theater.

Stanley, Diane, and Peter Vennema. *Charles Dickens: The Man Who Had Great Expectations.* Illustrated by Diane Stanley. New York: Morrow, 1993. Provides engaging information about the career and life of the nineteenth-century British novelist, whose realistic fictions with strong social concern are still influential today. Handsome pictures show the London Dickens discovered as a child and so profoundly described in many of his books.

Stanley, Diane, and Peter Vennema. *Cleopatra.* Illustrated by Diane Stanley. New York: Morrow, 1994. Drawing from many historical sources, the authors trace the life history of Cleopatra, the Queen of Egypt, whose name still glitters across history. Egyptian practices that made her queen, her relationships with the Roman generals Caesar and Antony, and their tragic failure and death are clearly explained. Mosaic-like pictures faithfully depict the practices and customs of the era.

Stanley, Jerry. *Children of the Dustbowl: The True Story of the School at Weedpatch Camp.* New York: Crown, 1992. The first section traces the plight of migrant workers' children during the Depression when their families moved from the Dust Bowl and traveled to California. Focus of the second part is on education and development of Weedpatch School. Stunning photographs and fine graphic design enhance the book's readability.

Sullivan, George. *In-Line Skating: A Complete Guide for Beginners.* New York: Cobblehill, 1993. A comprehensive guide to the popular new sport of the nineties. Information includes in-line skating's appeal, selection of skates, safety equipment, techniques, and tips for successful skating.

Swanson, Diane. *Safari Beneath the Sea: The Wonder World of the North Pacific Coast.* Photographs by the Royal British Columbia Museum. San Francisco: Sierra Club Books, 1994. Extraordinary underwater photographs show life beneath the sea, and highly descriptive language conveys detailed information about it. Chapters feature "Plants of Plenty," "Far-Out Fish," and "Mind-Boggling Mammals."

Terban, Marvin. *The Dove Dove: Funny Homograph Riddles.* Illustrated by Tom Huffman. New York: Clarion, 1988. Substitute homographs in seventy humorous, tricky riddles are presented. An excellent brain stretcher in the language arts curriculum.

Ventura, Piero. *Houses: Structures, Methods, and Ways of Living.* Boston: Houghton Mifflin, 1993. Detailed, captioned, and often amusing illustrations support the recounting of the history of houses. From cave dwellings to the modern apartment, readers learn how people constructed houses.

Walker, Barbara M. *The Little House Cookbook: Frontier Foods from Laura Ingalls Wilder's Classic Stories.* Illustrations by Garth Williams. New York: HarperCollins, 1979. Quotations from Wilder's original stories describing foods set the framework for this collection of recipes, which may be similar to ones used by the Ingalls family.

Walter, Mildred Pitts. *Mississippi Challenge.* New York: Bradbury, 1992. Describes the struggle for freedom and civil rights for black people in Mississippi, from the time of slavery to the signing of the Voting Rights Act in 1965. Using the voices of people involved whenever possible, the author weaves together an honest, faithful, and moving account of African-American history.

Waters, Kate. *Sarah Morton's Day: A Day in the Life of a Pilgrim Girl.* Photographs by Russ Kendall. New York: Scholastic, 1989. This photo essay, appropriate for primary-aged children, chronicles the life of a young girl in America in 1627.

Weekly Reader Staff. *Weekly Reader: 60 Years of News for Kids, 1928–1988.* New York: World Almanac, 1988. Selections of the major weekly school newspaper *Weekly Reader* between the years 1928 and 1988. Four pages are devoted to each year. Valuable source for modern history and current events studies.

Whiteley, Opal, and Jane Boulton. *Only Opal: The Diary of a Young Girl.* Illustrated by Barbara Cooney. New York: Philomel, 1994. A lyrical, poetic adaptation of the original writings of Opal Whiteley, an orphan girl who lived with a foster family in Oregon lumber camps at the turn of the century. Joyful watercolors echo Opal's simple but provocative words on longings for love, comforts in nature, and unfailing faith in life.

Wilcox, Charlotte. *A Skyscraper Story*. Photographs by Jerry Boucher. Minneapolis, MN: Carolrhoda Books, 1990. The book depicts all the elements involved in planning and constructing the Norwest Center in Minneapolis and describes the contributions of architects and engineers to the process. Photographs show the mathematical scale of the construction and the reliance on mathematical and geometric formulas.

Wilkinson, Philip. *Building*. Photographs by Dave King and Geoff Dann. New York: Knopf, 1995. This "Eyewitness" book describes various materials used in building such as bricks, earth, and stone and illustrates the different parts of a building like the floor, doors, and windows. An index is included.

Winter, Jeannette. *Follow the Drinking Gourd*. New York: Knopf, 1988. In bold pictures inspired by American folk art tradition and poetic words that weave together slave history and the song "The Drinking Gourd," the book presents the story of Peg Leg Joe and a group of runaway slaves who follow the Drinking Gourd and travel along the Underground Railroad north to freedom.

Yolen, Jane. *Encounter*. Illustrated by David Shannon. San Diego, CA: Harcourt Brace, 1992. A young Taino Indian boy on the island of San Salvador recounts the arrival of Christopher Columbus and the Spanish men; how he tries to warn his people not to welcome these strange, white visitors; and the later tragedy that happened to his tribe. Stunning paintings add to the dimension and depth of the story.

Yue, Charlotte, and David Yue. *Igloo*. Boston: Houghton Mifflin, 1988. Detailed description of how igloos are constructed and their functions in the lives of Inuit people. Information is also provided on the impact of the Arctic climate on Inuit culture and on changes occurring in Inuit society today.

Appendix:
Thematic Book
Collections

DISCOVERING WHAT SCIENTISTS DO
AND HOW THEY DO IT

Cobb, Vicki, and Josh Cobb. *Light Action! Amazing Experiments with Optics.* New York: HarperCollins, 1993.

Cobb, Vicki, and Kathy Darling. *Wanna Bet? Science Challenges to Fool You.* New York: Lothrop, Lee & Shepard, 1993.

Cone, Molly. *Come Back, Salmon.* San Francisco: Sierra Club Books, 1992.

Gibbons, Gail. *Spiders.* New York: Holiday House, 1993.

Giblin, James Cross. *The Riddle of the Rosetta Stone.* New York: Crowell, 1990.

Gold, Carol. *Science Express: 50 Scientific Stunts from the Ontario Science Centre.* Reading, MA: Addison-Wesley, 1991.

Lasky, Kathryn. *Dinosaur Dig.* New York: Morrow, 1990.

Lasky, Kathryn. *Surtsey: The Newest Place on Earth.* New York: Bradbury, 1992.

Lauber, Patricia. *The News about Dinosaurs.* New York: Bradbury, 1989.

Patent, Dorothy Hinshaw. *Where the Bald Eagles Gather.* New York: Clarion, 1984.

Lessem, Don. *Dinosaur Worlds: New Dinosaurs, New Discoveries.* Honesdale, PA: Boyds Mills Press, 1996.

Pringle, Laurence. *Living in a Risky World.* New York: Morrow, 1989.

Simon, Seymour. *New Questions and Answers about Dinosaurs.* New York: Morrow, 1990.

Smithsonian Institution. *Fun Machines: Step-by-Step Science Activity Projects from the Smithsonian Institution.* Milwaukee, WI: Gareth Stevens, 1993.

HOW WE CAN HELP SAVE THE ENVIRONMENT

Cherry, Lynne. *A River Ran Wild.* San Diego, CA: Harcourt Brace, 1993.

Cone, Molly. *Come Back, Salmon.* San Francisco: Sierra Club Books, 1992.

George, Jean Craighead. *The Wild, Wild Cookbook: A Guide for Young Wild-Food Foragers.* New York: Crowell, 1982.

Gibbons, Gail. *Nature's Green Umbrella: Tropical Rain Forests.* New York: Morrow, 1994.

Hendrich, Paula. *Saving America's Birds.* New York: Lothrop, Lee & Shepard, 1982.

Lasky, Kathryn. *Surtsey: The Newest Place On Earth.* New York: Hyperion, 1992.

Love, Ann, and Jane Drake. *Take Action: An Environmental Book for Kids.* New York: Morrow, 1992.

Pandell, Karen. *Land of Dark, Land of Light: The Arctic National Wildlife Refuge.* New York: Dutton, 1993.

Patent, Dorothy Hinshaw. *Where the Bald Eagles Gather.* New York: Clarion, 1984.

Pringle, Laurence. *Living in a Risky World.* New York: Morrow, 1989.

Stanley, Jerry. *Children of the Dustbowl: The True Story of the School at Weedpatch Camp.* New York: Crown, 1992.

IMMIGRATION

Bartone, Elisa. *American Too.* New York: Lothrop, Lee & Shepard, 1996.

Cohen, Barbara. *Molly's Pilgrim.* New York: Lothrop, Lee & Shepard, 1983.

Fisher, Leonard Everett. *Ellis Island.* New York: Holiday House, 1986.

Freedman, Russell. *Immigrant Kids.* New York: Dutton, 1980.

Goldish, Meish. *Immigration: How Should It Be Controlled?* New York: 21st Century Books, 1994.

Hoobler, Dorothy, and Thomas Hoobler. *The Italian American Family Album.* New York: Oxford University Press, 1994.

Say, Allen. *Grandfather's Journey.* New York: Houghton Mifflin, 1993.

THE LIVES OF CHILDREN ACROSS TIME AND PLACE

Ashabranner, Brent. *Born to the Land.* New York: Putnam, 1989.

Beirne, Barbara. *Siobhan's Journey: A Belfast Girl Visits the United States.* Minneapolis, MN: Carolrhoda Books, 1993.

Cohen, Barbara. *Molly's Pilgrim.* New York: Lothrop, Lee & Shepard, 1983.

Conrad, Pam. *Prairie Songs.* New York: HarperCollins, 1985.

Dorris, Michael. *Morning Girl.* New York: Hyperion, 1992.

Ekoomiak, Normee. *Arctic Memories.* New York: Holt, 1988.

Filiopovic, Zlata. *Zlata's Diary: A Child's Life in Sarajevo.* New York: Viking, 1994.

Freedman, Russell. *Immigrant Kids.* New York: Dutton, 1980.

Greenfield, Howard. *Hidden Children.* New York: Ticknor & Fields, 1993.

Hoobler, Dorothy, and Thomas Hoobler. *The Italian American Family Album.* New York: Oxford University Press, 1994.

Hopkinson, Deborah. *Sweet Clara and the Freedom Quilt.* New York: Knopf, 1993.

Kendall, Russ. *Eskimo Boy: Life in an Inupiaq Eskimo Village.* New York: Scholastic, 1992.

Lankford, Mary. *Hopscotch Around the World.* New York: Morrow, 1992.

Leigh, Nila. *Learning to Swim in Swaziland: A Child's-Eye View of a Southern African Country.* New York: Scholastic, 1993.

Levine, Ellen. *Freedom's Children: Young Civil Rights Activists Tell Their Own Stories.* New York: Putnam, 1993.

Lyons, Mary. *Letters from a Slave Girl.* New York: Scribner's, 1992.

McMahon, Patricia. *Chi-hoon: A Korean Girl.* Honesdale, PA: Boyds Mills Press, 1993.

Rosenberg, Maxine. *Hiding to Survive: Stories of Jewish Children Rescued from the Holocaust.* New York: Clarion, 1994.

Stanley, Jerry. *Children of the Dustbowl: The True Story of the School at Weedpatch Camp.* New York: Crown, 1992.

Whitely, Opal. *Only Opal: The Diary of a Young Girl.* New York: Philomel, 1994.

ALL THE CREATURES OF THE WORLD

Aliki. *My Visit to the Aquarium.* New York: HarperCollins, 1993.

Arnosky, Jim. *A Kettle of Hawks and Other Wildlife Groups.* New York: Lothrop, Lee & Shepard, 1990.

Brandenburg, Jim. *To the Top of the World: Adventures with Arctic Wolves.* New York: Walker, 1993.

Brandenburg, Jim. *Sand and Fog: Adventures in Southern Africa.* New York: Walker, 1994.

Brooks, Bruce. *Making Sense: Animal Perception and Communication.* New York: Farrar Straus Giroux, 1993.

Brown, Mary. *Wings Along the Waterway.* New York: Orchard, 1992.

Cone, Molly. *Come Back, Salmon.* San Francisco: Sierra Club Books, 1992.

Dunphy, Madeleine. *Here Is the Arctic Winter.* New York: Hyperion, 1993.

Gibbons, Gail. *Spiders.* New York: Holiday House, 1993.

Hendrich, Paula. *Saving America's Birds.* New York: Lothrop, Lee & Shepard, 1982.

Lacey, Elizabeth. *What's the Difference? A Guide to Some Familiar Animal Look-Alikes.* New York: Clarion, 1993.

Martin, James. *Hiding Out: Camouflage in the Wild.* New York: Crown, 1993.

Matthews, Downs. *Polar Bear Cubs.* New York: Simon and Schuster, 1989.

Matthews, Downs. *Arctic Summer.* New York: Simon and Schuster, 1993.

Melville, Herman. *Catskill Eagle.* New York: Philomel, 1991.

Morris, Desmond. *The World of Animals.* New York: Viking, 1993.

Pandell, Karen. *Land of Dark, Land of Light: The Arctic National Wildlife Refuge.* New York: Dutton, 1993.

Patent, Dorothy Hinshaw. *Where the Bald Eagles Gather.* New York: Clarion, 1984.

Patent, Dorothy Hinshaw. *Looking at Penguins.* New York: Holiday House, 1993.

Pringle, Laurence. *Antarctica: The Last Unspoiled Continent.* New York: Simon and Schuster, 1992.

Ryden, Hope. *America's Bald Eagle.* New York: Putnam, 1985.

Sattler, Helen Roney. *The Book of Eagles.* New York: Lothrop, Lee & Shepard, 1989.

Selsam, Millicent, and Joyce Hunt. *A First Look at Owls, Eagles, and Other Hunters of the Sky.* New York: Walker, 1986.

Simon, Seymour. *Wolves.* New York: HarperCollins, 1993.

SEEING YOURSELF AS A WRITER AND A LANGUAGE USER

Adler, David. *Remember Betsy Floss and Other Colonial American Riddles.* New York: Holiday House, 1987.

Cummings, Pat. *Talking with Artists.* New York: Bradbury, 1992.

Davis, Ossie. *Escape to Freedom: A Play about Young Frederick Douglass.* New York: Viking, 1978.

Eisenberg, Lisa, and Katy Hall. *Batty Riddles*. New York: Dial, 1993.

Fleischman, Paul. *Copier Creations*. New York: HarperCollins, 1993.

Granfield, Linda. *Extra! Extra! The Who, What, Where, When and Why of Newspapers*. New York: Orchard, 1993.

Leedy, Loreen. *The Furry News: How to Make a Newspaper*. New York: Holiday House, 1990.

Leedy, Loreen. *Messages in the Mailbox: How to Write a Letter*. New York: Holiday House, 1991.

Terban, Marvin. *The Dove Dove: Funny Homograph Riddles*. New York: Clarion, 1988.

Index

TY. TEXARKA